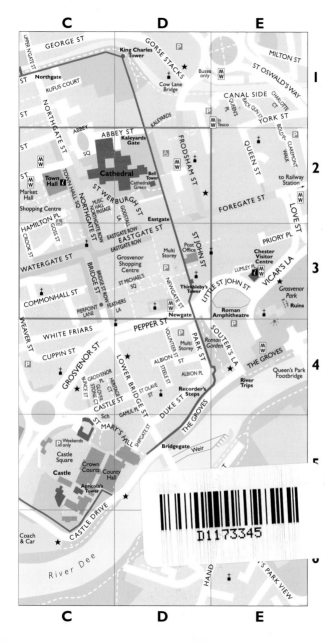

CHESTER

...MORE THAN A GUIDE

JARROLD
publishing

CHESTER...MORE THAN A GUIDE

JOHN MCILWAIN

CITY-BREAK GUIDES

Acknowledgements

Photography © Jarrold Publishing by Neil Jinkerson.

Additional photography by kind permission of: Catalyst, The Chester Grosvenor, Chester Zoo, Jodrell Bank, Laser Quest, David Mitchell, Tourism Development Unit.

The publishers wish to thank Alison Kelly (Chester City Council), Jane Ladyman (Chester Visitor Centre) and Joyce Rowlands (Blue Badge guide) for their invaluable assistance; also the many owners of Chester businesses for their kindness in allowing us to photograph their premises.

Designer:
Simon Borrough

Editor:
Angela Royston

Artwork and walk maps:
Clive Goodyer

City maps:
The Map Studio, Romsey, Hants. Main map based on cartography © George Philip Ltd

Front cover:
Stanley Palace

Previous page:
Chester Town Hall

Printed in Singapore.
ISBN 0 7117 2646 9 1/04

CONTENTS

WELCOME TO CHESTER

Chester is one of Britain's great cities, with a rich heritage drawn from 2,000 years of history. Here on the River Dee the Romans founded a garrison port, Deva, and occupied it for over 300 years. On the ruins of the Roman city, Saxons and then Normans built a new, larger town, gracing it with an abbey and fortifying it with a castle. Around it they built larger city walls, which proved so strong and impenetrable that they survive almost intact today. Next came the Rows, the half-timbered houses of medieval merchants, built over stone cellars and linked together by galleried walkways. In Tudor times, the abbey became a cathedral. Then Cromwell's cannon balls rained down on the city for 18 long months, causing much destruction and squalor in the 17th century.

Black-and-white architecture

But Chester recovered. During the next 200 years new streets were built in Georgian, classical and Gothic styles, until these styles were eclipsed by the Victorians' nostalgia for the medieval half-timbered style. Black-and-white was back! The purists may have winced, but Chester was now blessed with its own unique look. Today these well-preserved streets provide a romantic and historic

Left: The accordian man

Below: Bookland

backdrop to a plethora of sophisticated shops – a veritable shoppers' paradise.

Six million people visit the city each year. They come for the heritage, the shops, the lively atmosphere, and much more. For Chester is friendly: a sophisticated city with excellent shops, cafés and restaurants, and a commitment to good service. Chester is compact: within the city walls it's easy to find your way around. In summer, the city's street life is exhilarating, slightly wacky and always fun. Chester is a special place, much loved by those who live here and those who come to visit.

HIGHLIGHTS

Chester and its surrounding area has so much to offer that a short stay will probably leave you planning your next visit! But a few days is all that most of us have. To help you make the most of your time here, this section recommends the absolute unmissables, many of which, in Chester, are free.

THE ROWS
Eastgate Street, Bridge Street, Watergate Street; map C3–D3
Chester's Rows, black-and-white 'double-decker' streets, are unique to the city. The ancient galleried shops, containing some of the oldest frontages in England, act as a magnet drawing visitors to Chester from all over the world. The shops themselves are superb and individual, and their arrangement on two levels generates an energetic and lively street life, with lots of buskers (anything from bagpipes to Beethoven) and street theatre (everything from living statues to stilt-walkers).

A WALK AROUND THE CITY WALLS
Marked in red on the map
Chester's city walls are certainly the finest in Britain. In the north and east they follow the line of the old Roman walls. Other places in Britain have city

Bridge Street

The city walls

E N E R G E T I C W I S H
The wishing steps which link the south and east walls were built in 1785. To make your wish come true you have to run up and down the steps without drawing breath. If you try this, have page 95 of this book open – the location of emergency medical services!

walls, but none are as complete, as accessible and as walkable as Chester's. You can join the walls at many places, and some sections are accessible to wheelchairs. A brisk hour's walk will take you right around the entire walls. What's more, as you go you'll see virtually all the features which make Chester such a superb place to spend time in.

First, there's the cathedral with its lovely gardens and Georgian close; then far below is the canal in its cutting, with historic towers looming above; next it's the Roodee, the ancient bowl of a race-course and, beyond, views to the hills of Wales. From there the wall descends to Chester Castle, then climbs again to give you a grandstand view of the River Dee and the boaty things that always seem to be going on there. Finally, it's up past historic black-and-white houses to Eastgate Arch with its world-famous ironwork clock, and that amazing view of Chester's bustling Rows below.

Open: 24 hours a day, 365 days a year
Entry: free
Further information: pages 35–36

CHESTER CATHEDRAL
Abbey Square; map C2

This massive medieval sandstone church stands in the heart of the city, a stone's throw from the Town Hall and the Rows. Formerly St Werburgh's Abbey, it was transformed into a cathedral in the 1540s, but remains one of England's best-preserved examples of a Benedictine abbey. There are several reasons why you should see the cathedral. For one thing it's very ancient and truly lovely to look at. The most intriguing part is the choir, with its magnificent stalls carved in 1380 – look out for the elephant (see page 32). There are also some wonderful stained-glass windows. Another reason for spending time here is that, amid the bustle of the city, it is a delightful and cool place just to sit, think, say a prayer or light a candle. Outside, the cloisters are particularly peaceful, as is the cathedral green near the belltower.

Westminster window, Chester Cathedral

There are two further, unexpected reasons why you might want to visit Chester Cathedral. In the ancient undercroft are an excellent café in the historic and lofty monks' refectory (see page 34) and a shop selling gifts and books – some superb souvenirs here.

Open: daily, 8.00–18.00
Entry: free, but a donation is requested
Further information: pages 32–34

The nave, Chester Cathedral

> ### HALLELUJAH!
> Popular legend has it that George Frederick Handel composed some of his *Messiah* in Chester Cathedral, while awaiting a packet-boat to take him to Ireland.

Eastgate Street

TREAT YOURSELF

Buy yourself some super soap or a fancy face wash at Lush near Eastgate Arch (map D3). All their soap is made from natural ingredients, and is cut and weighed to your requirements. Even if you buy nothing, enjoy the perfumed atmosphere!

EASTGATE ARCH
Eastgate Street; map D2

Even if you can't face walking right round the walls then at least climb the steps to Eastgate Arch, with its wonderful photogenic clock and its exciting view of Eastgate Street below. The ironwork clock you walk beneath is over 100 years old, originally conceived to celebrate Queen Victoria's Diamond Jubilee in 1897 but completed somewhat late – two years late in fact, in time for the sovereign's 80th birthday.

Open: 24 hours a day, 365 days a year
Entry: free
Further information: pages 37–38

River Dee

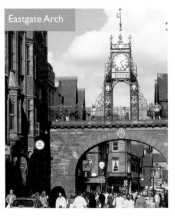
Eastgate Arch

ROMAN RUBBISH

The Rows coincide with the area of the old Roman garrison. The piled-up debris from Roman buildings meant that the back doors of the living quarters were at ground level.

RIVER DEE

No visit to Chester would be complete without a walk along the riverside. The River Dee, once the city's commercial artery and its main defence against Welsh attack in medieval times, is now a delightful summer playground. Just a few minutes' walk down from the city centre are The Groves (map D5–E4), a tree-lined promenade alongside the rippling Dee. Here you can stroll along the river to the suspension bridge – the Queen's Park Footbridge – and the Old Dee Bridge and back again. Or you can take to the water – if you're feeling energetic, why not hire a rowing boat? Alternatively, you can join one of the pleasure boats on a tour (see page 83). Or you can just sit and watch other people doing these things. Better still, give yourself an excuse to linger – wander up to the Boathouse pub or the delightfully retro Blue Moon Café (see page 69) for a drink or a meal.

Blue Moon Café

CHESTER ZOO
Caughall Road, Upton

Britain's most visited zoo is very different from most zoos. Mr Mottershead founded it in 1903, at Upton on the outskirts of Chester, on the principle that animals need plenty of space. The 7,000 animals here have certainly got this in their generously-sized enclosures amid attractive, landscaped gardens. It's no wonder that over a million people come here each year. Conservation is important at Chester Zoo, and many species here are bred with the aim of returning more animals to the wild. The zoo prides itself on innovation and one unusual feature is the Zoofari Overhead Railway which glides at treetop height amongst the animals. The latest major development is the amazing Spirit of the Jaguar, with its recreated grassy savannah and rainforest environments complete with sounds and smells.

Getting there: regular buses from Town Hall Bus Exchange (map C2)
Open: daily from 10.00; closing times vary throughout the year – ring to check. Closed 25 Dec
Entry: about £10
Tel: 01244 380280
Further information: pages 34–35

Chester Zoo

THE GROSVENOR MUSEUM
Grosvenor Street; map C4

A visit to The Grosvenor Museum is a great way to put Chester in its historical perspective. It has three floors of interesting exhibits, covering not just the city's history but local wildlife and art too. There's a strong hands-on accent, with many kinds of interactive displays. Jewels in the crown are the Roman tombstones, the real Georgian house, the Timeline Gallery and the marvellous Silver Gallery, which includes the superb Chester race cups. You could round off a morning here with lunch at, for example, Ego, Franc's or Pastarazzi (see pages 70 and 73).

Open: daily; Mon–Sat 10.30–17.00, Sun 13.00–16.00
Entry: free, but donations welcomed
Further information: page 40

TOWN HALL
Town Hall Square; map C2

It's impossible to miss Chester's fine Town Hall in the centre of the city. This high, Victorian Gothic building was opened by the future King Edward VII in 1869. The interior is impressive too, but, apart from the Tourist Information Centre on the ground floor, it is not open to visitors.

In front of the Town Hall is Stephen Broadbent's sculpture *The Celebration of Chester*. This elegant statue was commissioned jointly in 1992 by the City Council, Chester Cathedral and Capital Bank and represents the coming together of three driving forces – thanksgiving, protection and industry.

The Celebration of Chester

THE GROSVENORS AND CHESTER

You won't go far in Chester without bumping into the name 'Grosvenor' – Grosvenor Park, the Grosvenor Hotel, The Grosvenor Museum, to name but a few. What's it all about?

Silver Gallery, The Grosvenor Museum

Statue of Hugh Lupus Grosvenor, 1st Duke of Westminister

Grosvenor Bridge

The Grosvenor family is one of the wealthiest in England, with their country seat, Eaton Hall, located at Eccleston, just 3 kilometres (2 miles) up the river from Chester. The Grosvenors can be traced back almost a thousand years to the Norman Conquest, when William the Conqueror made his nephew Hugh d'Avranches (known as Hugh Lupus) the first Earl of Chester, giving him most of the land in Cheshire. Hugh's nephew was Gilbert Grosvenor (*le gros veneur* meant 'master of the hunt').

For several centuries the Grosvenors ruled locally, fought for various kings and extended their fortunes by marrying shrewdly. One such marriage, around 1443, was to Joan of Eaton, heiress to the Eaton estate, which eventually became the Grosvenor seat. The family also had mining interests in Wales.

The Grosvenors' enduring links with Chester were cemented by Sir Richard Grosvenor (1585–1645), the first Baronet, a diligent and educated man who became MP for the city, setting the pattern for over two centuries.

CHANGING HALLS

From a simple Tudor building, Eaton Hall underwent several transformations. One critic called the 1814 incarnation 'a vast pile of mongrel Gothic'. A guest, dining in the new, vaulted breakfast room in 1883, exclaimed, 'Good God! I never expected to eat bacon and eggs in a cathedral!' The current Eaton Hall is much more modest.

Sir Thomas Grosvenor (1655–1700), Mayor of Chester and long-serving MP, having planned a grand new Eaton Hall, married Mary Davies, heiress to farmland on the outskirts of London. This land was called Mayfair and Belgravia, now some of the most expensive land in the world! In the 18th and 19th centuries, income from the Welsh mines allowed the Grosvenors to build the elegant houses associated with these fashionable London districts.

The family's wealth, prestige and influence grew, and in 1874 Hugh Lupus Grosvenor was made 1st Duke of Westminster. Hugh's immense wealth was matched by his philanthropy. He was involved in countless charitable works in London, Cheshire and North Wales, and it is principally to him that Chester owes many of its public buildings, open spaces, churches and schools. The Grosvenor's relationship with Chester – and the family's generosity – continues into the 21st century.

The Grosvenor Museum

PLANNING YOUR VISIT

With so much to see and do it's a good idea to plan your visit carefully to get the most out of it. Here are some suggestions for things to do in one day, or two or three. You don't have to do them all, or in any set order – they are definitely pick-and-mix!

WHAT TO DO IN ONE DAY

Wander round the cathedral. The first service is held at 7.30 on weekdays and it opens for visitors at 8.00. Allow at least 30 to 45 minutes to see the cathedral.

For most visitors, no day in Chester is complete without some shopping. You could follow the Shoppers' Walk described on pages 26–27 or, if you want to be more selective, look at the shopping section on pages 57–67.

EVENSONG AT CHESTER CATHEDRAL

You don't have to be a church-goer and it need not cost you any money (but you are requested to make a donation on your way out). Just take a pew in the ancient choirstalls and let the superb singing echo around you. Mon–Fri 17.30, Saturdays 16.15, Sundays 15.30.

Don't miss the Town Crier's booming proclamations at the Cross (map C3). He (or she!) gives you the time of day at midday on Tuesdays to Saturdays in summer. Be there to join in the 500-year-old tradition.

A combined bus and river tour (see page 83) will help you to get your bearings and give you a taste of the delightful atmosphere on the River Dee. Allow an hour and a half.

Another way to get an overview of the city is to walk along the walls. The full circuit is only 3 kilometres (2 miles) but allow between one and two hours, depending on how fast you walk. If you want to do just a single stretch, start at Northgate Arch (map C1) and walk clockwise to the Eastgate Arch (map D2). Here you can leave the walls to visit the shops (see pages 57–67) or carry on to Newgate and Chester Visitor Centre for tea or coffee (map E3). Besides masses of information for visitors and a gift shop, the Visitor Centre has an introductory DVD presentation, 'A Place for All Seasons'. You can continue on to the river at The Groves (map D5–E4) and come back through the Roman Garden (see page 44).

For lunch, Dutton's (see page 74) is a good bet, or, for something more leisurely, try Chez Jules or Franc's (see page 70 for both). If time is limited, you can grab a ciabatta at Alfresco (see page 68) or a crêpe from Gabby's (see page 69) and eat outdoors.

The Grosvenor Museum (see page 40) is well worth a visit, if only to see the Roman exhibits on the ground floor, but the Georgian house and the first floor silver are spectacular too.

Chester Visitor Centre

Alfresco

WHAT TO DO IN THE NEXT TWO OR THREE DAYS

One option for a two- or three-day stay is to follow the one-day suggestions but do them at a more leisurely pace. Walk the whole of the walls, try two or three of the lunch venues, stroll round The Grosvenor Museum, shop till you drop! What else you do depends largely on your own taste and interests. Here are some suggestions to choose from. For ideas of what to do in the evening have a look at pages 80–81.

The Grosvenor Museum

A DAY AT THE RACES

Why not treat yourself to a day at the races? Chester's racecourse is special: a spectacular, tight circle of green between the city walls and the river. Highlights of the year are the May Festival (the biggest), Roman race day in June (the most spectacular), the July meeting (the most social) and the August Festival (which includes the biggest family fun day of any racecourse in Britain).

Further information: page 84.

Guided walks

Try a Pastfinder walk and learn more about the city. Guided walks start from the Chester Visitor Centre and the Town Hall Tourist Information Centre (see page 28). They take about an hour and a half each. In summer, you can clank round the town with a Roman soldier in full battle gear (see page 82). Or you could follow one of the walks suggested on pages 23–29.

Chester races

River boat

Grosvenor Park

If you have time to spare, you might choose to spend it in Grosvenor Park (see page 41), a delightful green haven full of flowers in summer and just a stone's throw from the river. After you've visited the park, stroll down to the river for a leisurely coffee (or lunch) at the wonderfully nostalgic Blue Moon Café (see page 69).

Cheshire Military Museum

Drop into the Cheshire Military Museum at Chester Castle (see page 30). It's modern, interactive and not too military!

Out of town

Venturing further afield, Eaton Hall, the family seat of the Grosvenors, is just 5 kilometres (3 miles) up the river. What

better way to visit it than by boat? Bithell Boats (see page 83) do a very pleasant two-hour cruise upstream through the Eaton estate.

Chester Zoo is the largest and most spacious zoo in Britain (see page 34). Animal-lovers really need a full day to do it justice, but, if you choose the animals you most want to see, you could get round in about three hours.

If you're a dedicated shopper, you should fit in a visit to Cheshire Oaks at Ellesmere (see page 58). It is Europe's biggest designer outlet, and only a few miles from the city.

For more suggestions on places to visit near Chester, see pages 88–89.

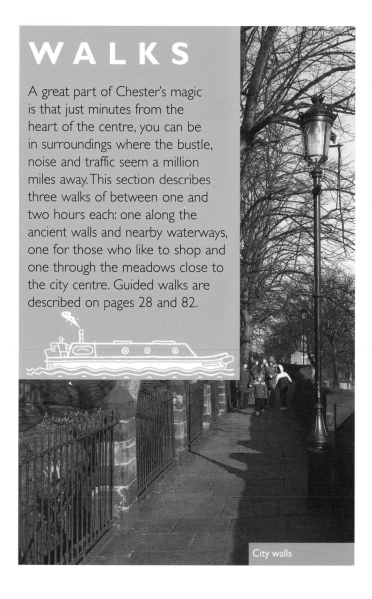

WALKS

A great part of Chester's magic is that just minutes from the heart of the centre, you can be in surroundings where the bustle, noise and traffic seem a million miles away. This section describes three walks of between one and two hours each: one along the ancient walls and nearby waterways, one for those who like to shop and one through the meadows close to the city centre. Guided walks are described on pages 28 and 82.

City walls

WATER AND WALLS WALK

This walk includes Chester's canal locks, the riverside racecourse and a stretch of city walls as well. It's important to note that the racecourse part of the walk is closed on race days.

Join the city wall at the Eastgate Arch and go north past the cathedral's east end. Descend to cobbled Abbey Street and go under the wall through Kaleyards Gate (see page 36). Cross the car park, bearing left into Frodsham Street. At the Slow Boat restaurant, go down steps and left onto the towpath of the Shropshire Union Canal. Follow the towpath through a long wooded cutting, with the city walls high above you on their sandstone cliffs.

In the shadow of the concrete bridge carrying St Martin's Way, cross the footbridge. Ahead is the last bit of Canal Street. Turn left, crossing the railway and left again into Raymond Street. Almost opposite, take the entry road down to Tower Wharf. Here you'll find Telford's Warehouse, a good place for coffee or a snack while watching the boats. Cross the white-painted iron 'roving' bridge ahead. Returning on the other side of the basin, look for a second stretch of canal below on your right. Via steps down the bank, join the lower canal's towpath going under the road. Follow the canal round a sharp right-hand bend. Past the boat-shaped Scout HQ, you'll see a lifting bridge. Cross it

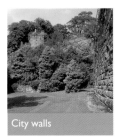
City walls

and follow the canal to busy New Crane Street. Turn left for about 300 metres (330 yards). On race days, or as a short cut, follow New Crane Street, Watergate Street and Eastgate Street back to your starting point.

On non-race days, cross the road and immediately follow a concrete track down the far side of the railway arches, with a view of the racecourse on your left. At the river, keep left

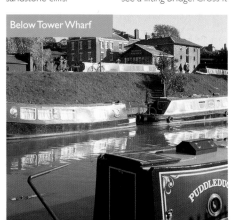
Below Tower Wharf

ELECTRICITY FROM THE RIVER DEE
Chester was the first British city to use hydro-electric power, generated by turbines in a power station by Old Dee Bridge.

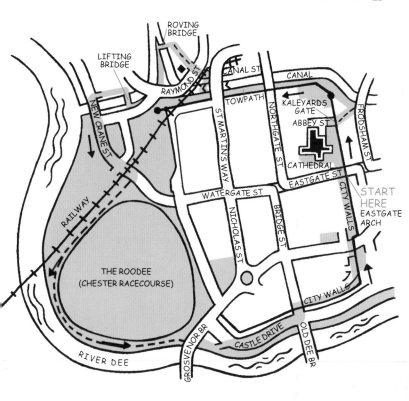

ROVING
BRIDGE

LIFTING
BRIDGE

RAYMOND ST

CANAL ST

CANAL

NEW CRANE ST

TOWPATH

KALEYARDS
GATE

ABBEY ST

FRODSHAM ST

ST MARTIN'S WAY

NORTHGATE ST

CATHEDRAL

EASTGATE ST

RAILWAY

WATERGATE ST

BRIDGE ST

CITY WALLS

START
HERE
EASTGATE
ARCH

NICHOLAS ST

THE ROODEE
(CHESTER RACECOURSE)

CITY WALLS

GROSVENOR BR

CASTLE DRIVE

OLD DEE BR

RIVER DEE

and shortly pick up the raised concrete track round the racecourse. Follow the riverbank back to the city, under Grosvenor Bridge, along Castle Drive, past Old Dee Bridge. Climb Recorder Steps (look for the plaque dated 1700) to the city walls. Follow it anticlockwise and uphill back to Eastgate Arch.

Narrowboats at Northgate Locks

SHOPPERS' WALK

Start at the Town Hall and turn right into Northgate Street. At the junction with Eastgate Street, turn right past the Cross to explore Watergate Street (see page 58). Shopping in the Rows is a double delight, so as you go down the right-hand side of the street, keep an eye on the street-level shops on the left, in case you want to inspect them on the way back. Cross to Ye Olde Custom House Inn and return up Watergate Street at first-floor (Rows) level. Look out for Sofa Workshop (see page 64). On returning to the Cross, go down to street level, turn right and wander down Bridge Street. Look out for Bookland, with its crypt (see page 53). At the bottom, cross over and return at Rows level. You'll pass The Rather Nice Card Shop (see page 67).

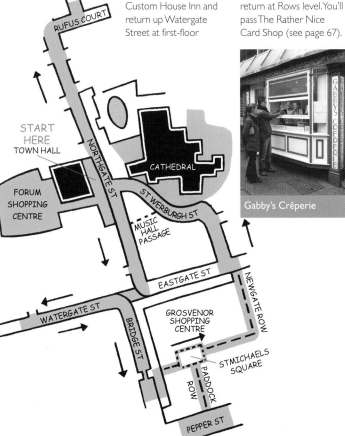

Gabby's Crêperie

RUFUS COURT

START HERE
TOWN HALL

NORTHGATE ST

CATHEDRAL

FORUM SHOPPING CENTRE

ST WERBURGH ST

MUSIC HALL PASSAGE

EASTGATE ST

NEWGATE ROW

WATERGATE ST

BRIDGE ST

GROSVENOR SHOPPING CENTRE

ST MICHAELS SQUARE

PADDOCK ROW

PEPPER ST

Grosvenor Shopping Centre

Street is a great place for light snacks (see page 68), or, if you fancy the open air, grab a crêpe from Gabby's Crêperie in Music Hall Passage behind St Werburgh Row, and sit and eat it on Cathedral Green on a sunny day.

To finish the walk, continue up St Werburgh's Row back to the Town Hall. If you're not shopped out by now, to the side of the Town Hall is the Forum Shopping Centre which leads into the colourful indoor city market. You could also check out Northgate Street and Rufus Court (see page 58) on the right at the top of the street.

Halfway up, turn right into the Grosvenor Shopping Centre – an elegant, lofty, white stone arcade. You may like to stop at the café space known as St Michael's Square for coffee while you ponder your next move. If you're interested in furniture and furnishings, turn right into Paddock Row. Down the escalator at the end there are several shops in Pepper Street. Otherwise, from St Michael's Square, go straight on, bearing left with the flow via Newgate Row to Eastgate Street.

From here you can explore Eastgate Street in either direction, but if you do, return to the Grosvenor Shopping Centre exit, cross Eastgate Street into St Werburgh Street and walk up towards the cathedral.

There are two good choices for lunch here. Alfresco in St Werburgh

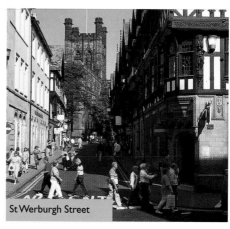

St Werburgh Street

RIVERSIDE WALK

This walk takes you away from the city to the open meadows on the far side of the Dee. It can sometimes be muddy, so bear this in mind in your choice of footwear.

Start at Newgate (map D3). Meander down through the nearby Roman Garden to the River Dee. Turn right along The Groves until you come to the weir and Old Dee Bridge. Cross the river by the bridge and, on the far side, go left beneath a block of flats. Follow the riverbank path below the Bank of Scotland building, underneath the suspension bridge and past the backs of the stylish Victorian

villas in Queen's Park. Eventually, at a gate, you'll enter open meadows.

As you walk along the riverbank, thank Mr and Mrs Brown for giving Earl's Eye meadows to the people of Chester in 1929. Ahead of you, the river describes a huge arc to the right, with elegant houses of various heights and styles on the wooded bluffs of Boughton. Follow the riverside path round until you are opposite the moorings for Chester Sailing Club. Just before a gateway, take the path to your right.

Walk by the side of a ditch up to Bottoms Lane. Follow this to the top, where the road forks at

Bandstand, The Groves

the railings of a school playing field. Bear along St George's Crescent. Where you meet Queen's Park Road, cross over, heading right, then go immediately left into Victoria Crescent. This curves round towards the river. Keep a lookout for the suspension bridge on your right, for it will take you across the Dee to The Groves, within sight of your starting point.

GUIDED WALKS

To learn more about the city as you walk, join a Pastfinder guided walk from the Town Hall. Tours start at 10.30 (and 14.15 in summer) from the Chester Visitor Centre (map E3), and 10.45 (and 14.30 in summer) from the Tourist Information Centre at the Town Hall (map C2).

Canoes on the Dee

Queen's Park
Footbridge

Key Tours are a new
venture. On a few
summer days, they give
you a chance to look
beyond some of Chester's
normally locked doors –
in the city walls' towers,
for example. Key Tours
can also be pre-arranged.
Ring 01244 402445 for
more details.

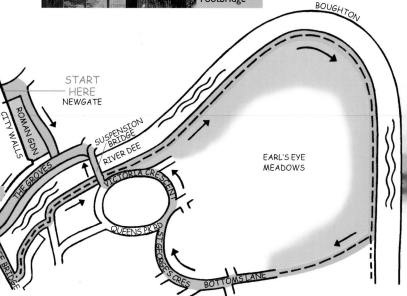

BOUGHTON

START
HERE
NEWGATE

CITY WALLS

ROMAN GDN

SUSPENSION
BRIDGE

RIVER DEE

THE GROVES

VICTORIA CRESCENT

EARL'S EYE
MEADOWS

QUEENS PK RD

ST GEORGE'S CRES

BOTTOMS LANE

E BRIDGE

SIGHTSEEING

There is plenty to explore and enjoy in Chester: the splendid Rows, the city walls, the beautiful riverside, two fine museums, to name just a few. And all of these are free of charge! The cathedral's free too (but it is suggested you make a donation). This section describes all the main sites you might wish to visit.

Cheshire Military Museum
Castle Square; map C5

This modern, exciting little museum comes as a surprise. Even if you're not military-minded, there are many things here to arouse your interest. Cheshire has always been a strong army county, and the museum commemorates the history, right up to the present day, of the 22nd Cheshire Regiment and other army units connected with the county. Throughout, though, you gain a wider perspective on historical events and life in different eras.

Everything is imaginatively presented and explained with many visual and aural treats: figures to touch, graphic displays, medals, audios of veterans talking about going into action, the role of army wives, reminiscences of National Service, and even embroideries sewn by convalescing soldiers. There's a strong accent on interactive displays, which children will enjoy.

DON'T MISS
The oldest real army uniform in existence in the country.

Cheshire Military Museum

> **VICTORIA CROSS**
> In 1916 Private 'Todger' Jones, of the Cheshire Regiment, managed to capture 102 Germans single-handed. The Victoria Cross he won for his bravery is on display in the Cheshire Military Museum.

The Litani tableau: Litani is in Syria, and the Cheshires were the last regiment to go into action on horseback.

The World War I interactive displays. The pens with which the Japanese signed their surrender in 1945.

Open: daily; 10.00–17.00 (last entry 16.30). Closed 22 Dec–2 Jan
Entry: under £5
Tel: 01244 327617
Website:
www.chester.ac.uk/militarymuseum
Disabled access: limited

Agricola Tower

Chester Castle
Castle Square; map C5

Little remains of the castle that the Normans built here from 1070 onward. It was a typical motte and bailey affair with a mound and a keep. The baileys were the inner and outer walled courtyards. From 1788 to 1822 Thomas Harrison knocked most of the castle down to build a shire hall, law courts, a jail and a barracks – the buildings we see today. The only significant survival is the Agricola Tower which dates from around the end of the 12th century. Visiting is restricted and you're advised to inquire in advance through the Visitor Services Officer at The Grosvenor Museum.
Entry: free to exterior
Tel: 01244 402008

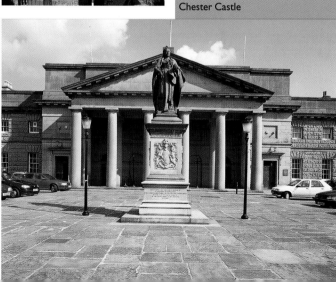

Chester Castle

The Chester Pilgrim

The Elephant
and Castle

Chapel of St Werburgh

Choir stalls

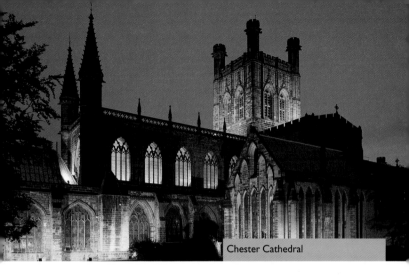

Chester Cathedral

Chester Cathedral
Abbey Square; map C2

This grand sandstone building occupies a central place in the city. Churches have stood on the site for around 1,400 years; after the Romans left, the Saxons built a succession of ever-bigger churches, culminating in a 10th-century minster to house the relics of St Werburgh. But here, as elsewhere, the Normans transformed things. In 1092 Hugh Lupus, the first Norman Earl of Chester and a nephew of William the Conqueror, founded a Benedictine abbey. The monks' quarters were built first, and most of today's church was constructed between 1250 and 1500. The bad news was that no sooner was the church finished than King Henry VIII dissolved the monastery (along with others up and down the land). The good news, however, was that the buildings survived to become, in 1541, the cathedral of the new diocese of Chester.

DON'T MISS

The west window (1961), which portrays the Holy Family surrounded by northern saints.

The choir stalls (1380): one of the finest examples of medieval carving in Britain. While you're there, look for the elephant and castle – the 14th-century carver would never have seen an elephant. It's on the north side of the choir.

The north transept, the oldest part of the cathedral, dating from around 1100. Look for the cobweb picture – in a modest niche, this 150-year-old painting of Mary and the Christ-child is actually painted on a web.

The consistory court (1636): here ecclesiastical trials took place – concerning perhaps the ownership of property or family disputes, or clergy accused of heresy or immorality.

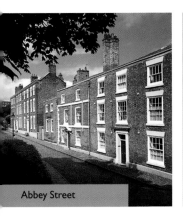
Abbey Street

PUNISHMENT FOR HERESY

In 1555, during the reign of Queen Mary Tudor, George Marsh, a widower with children, was tried for heresy at the cathedral's consistory court because he had preached Luther's (Protestant) doctrine. He was sentenced to death and, reading his Bible, he was led to Gallows Hill in Boughton, where he was burned at the stake.

St Werburgh's shrine in the Lady Chapel (*c.* 1340): this is where the saint's relics were kept. In the Middle Ages thousands of pilgrims flocked to such shrines to be blessed or healed.

The modern refectory west window (2000) depicts the Creation in all its glorious forms. Amongst many depictions, look for the DNA double helix, the brain scan and the skyscrapers.

You're hardly likely to miss the excellent cathedral shop as you enter and leave through the 12th-century undercroft. Here you'll find many attractive gifts, souvenirs and books.
Open: visitors' entrance open daily from 8.00–18.00
Entry: free, but a donation is requested
Tel: 01244 324756
Website: www.chestercathedral.com
Disabled access: full
Other facilities: restaurant and shop

Chester Zoo
Caughall Road, Upton
Over a million people a year visit Chester Zoo, only a few minutes north of the city centre. One of Europe's top zoos, it is famous for its large enclosures and attractively landscaped gardens. In its 100-year history, the mission here has always been to give animals the space they need to thrive, and Chester has constantly been a leader in the conservation of rare and endangered species.

It's worth looking out for details of the talks which keepers give about the animals in their care. These days the zoo has 7,000 animals encompassing 500 species. You'll be lucky to see all these in just one day's visit but, if possible …

DON'T MISS
The National Elephant Centre with its herd of Asian elephants.
The Spirit of the Jaguar savannah and rainforest environments.

The Chimpanzee Forest.
The Twilight Zone, where day becomes night and 200 bats fly free.
Dragons in Danger.
Tsavo, the Black Rhino Experience.
The Zoofari Overhead Railway, an extra treat, allowing you a bird's-eye view of many enclosures.

Getting there: regular buses from Town Hall Bus Exchange (map C2)

Open: daily from 10.00; closing times vary throughout the year – ring to check. Closed 25 Dec

Entry: about £10

Tel: 01244 380280

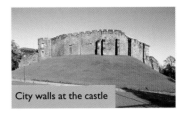
City walls at the castle

Website:
www.chesterzoo.org

Disabled access: almost full; wheelchairs for hire as well as five electric scooters, but book in advance.

City walls
Marked in red on the map

A prime reason why so many visitors return to Chester is its superb city walls. Few places boast walls as ancient or as complete as these. What makes them doubly special is the elevated walkway which lets you stroll for 3 kilometres (2 miles) right around the city, enjoying privileged glimpses in some places, superb views in others. Allow one to two hours to walk all the way round. Access points are plentiful.

The Romans built wooden walls and deep ditches to keep marauding locals out of their garrison. In the Middle Ages these became the foundations of the east and north sections we see today. The rest of the walls were a 12th-century extension which took in Chester Castle, while medieval watch towers strengthed the fortifications.

During the English Civil War (1642–46) the walls (and the rest of the city) were

Chester Zoo

AVOIDING GUNFIRE
King Charles I watched his troops
fighting (and losing) from the
walls. When things got rather
hot, he retreated to the cathedral
tower, where a bullet from a
sniper nearly killed him.

pounded by Cromwell's guns for 18
months, as his Parliamentarian troops
tried to get into the city, which had
remained loyal to King Charles I. The
king on one occasion stood on Phoenix
Tower, now known as King Charles's
Tower, watching his army being beaten
at nearby Rowton Moor. The most
complete of the medieval towers, it
bears a plaque marked 1613 and a
carved phoenix, emblem of the medieval
guild which met here.

King Charles's Tower

Bonewaldesthorne's Tower, in the north-
western corner, originally played its part
in the defences, but was left high and dry
by the 14th century as the River Dee
silted up. It was succeeded by the Water
Tower, but this too became stranded.

DON'T MISS

The section of original Roman walls
on the outside of the walls just south
of Kaleyards Gate (map D2) at the end
of Abbey Street.
The view from the walls of the elegant
Georgian houses of the cathedral close.
The River Dee viewed from the walls
below Newgate.
The view of the racecourse from Nuns
Road (at the spot where the wall
descends to street level).
The views of the Welsh hills from the
north-western section of the walls.
Emerging at rooftop height to look down
on bustling Eastgate Street (see page 38).

**STILL PROTECTING
THE CITY**
The monks of St Werburgh's
Abbey (now the cathedral) had
a long trek to reach their
kitchen garden (kaleyard) via
Eastgate until Edward I gave
permission in 1275 for a small
gate to be made in the wall.
Kaleyards Gate was duly
opened, but it is still locked at
dusk, by King Edward's order,
to protect the city.

Roman soldier

Afterwards, there's a hands-on studio where you can play Roman games and kids can try on a Roman centurion's helmet and breastplate.

In case you're wondering why Dewa is spelt with a 'w' and not a 'v', as in the Roman name Deva, it's because that's the way the Romans pronounced it. One more thing – look out for Roman patrols when you're in the town. If you see a squad of children marching in formation, they're almost certainly from Dewa Roman Experience.

Open: daily 9.00–17.00. Closed 25 and 26 Dec
Entry: under £5
Tel: 01244 343407
Disabled access: limited
Other facilities: gift shop

Seeing the Shropshire Union Canal in its sandstone gorge, way below the northern part of the walls.

Open: 24 hours a day, 365 days a year
Entry: free

Dewa Roman Experience
Pierpoint Lane, off Bridge Street; map C3

Although Chester has such a rich Roman heritage, much of the original fortress is hidden under the modern city. Even those bits that are technically visible are often inaccessible. At Dewa Roman Experience you get a rare chance to see a substantial chunk of real Roman foundations, revealing 2,000 years of history. Before that, you step aboard a Roman galley, then experience the sights, sounds (and smells) of life in a Roman fortress.

Eastgate Arch
Eastgate Street; map D2

The distinctive ironwork clock in Chester's Eastgate Street is probably the second most-photographed in the world after Big Ben in London. The stone arch beneath it stands where two great gates once stood. The first, with two massive stone arches and flanking towers, was built by the Romans to guard the main road from London and York. The second, built in the Middle Ages, had two octagonal towers each four storeys high. These were demolished in 1766 to make way, soon after, for the present arch which preserved the circuit of the city walls.

The clock did not arrive until 1899. OK, so the date on it is 1897, but it was two years late in the making and was set ticking on Queen Victoria's 80th birthday rather than on her Diamond Jubilee. The overall design was by John Douglas, one of Chester's two famous architects and the man who created the city's black-and-white architectural style.

Eastgate Street
Map D3

Eastgate Street

Eastgate Street has been Chester's main thoroughfare for nearly 2,000 years. The Roman's *Via Principalis* was around 2 metres (6 feet) below the present level of the street. Today, the street includes three prominent features that represent a cross section of life in Chester through the ages:

High Cross

As you would expect, the High Cross, at the west end of Eastgate Street, was originally a religious monument, probably adorned with the figures of saints, apostles and the Virgin Mary. As the place where the four main Roman streets met, the Cross was and is the focal point of Chester's open-air life. It is a natural assembly point – the place for markets, meetings and mystery plays, the spot where wrongdoers were pelted with rotten eggs and fruit as they sat in the stocks or stood in the pillory. The actual cross was removed when Cromwell's troops finally broke into the town in 1646. With a few original parts rescued from unlikely places it was reconstructed in 1949 in the Roman Garden, but returned to the city centre in 1975. Each May during the Folk Festival (see page 84), the Cross is dressed with flowers.

The Boot Inn

This pub is one of Chester's oldest. The building originally belonged to a medieval merchant, but the timber frame we see today at Row level dates from around the time it opened as a pub – 1643. The façade was rebuilt and restored in the late 19th century and again in 1988. Until that year, the actual pub had been tucked away at the back, with a barber's shop at the front. Before that, there is thought to have been a brothel here.

High Cross

Architectural diversity in Eastgate Street

Architecture

Take a good look at Browns of Chester (now Debenhams) and also the buildings on either side of it. Here in a nutshell is the battle of architectural styles that raged in Chester in the 19th century. Until the 1820s Eastgate was a street of modest Georgian façades. The classical revival had struck elsewhere in the town, with Thomas Harrison's rebuilding of the castle being the prime example. In 1828 it came to Eastgate Street in the form of No. 34 (Browns of Chester). Then came the fashion for neo-Gothic, represented by Thomas Penson's 'crypt building' of 1858, built on the left of Browns over an unspoilt medieval cellar. By 1860 both styles were eclipsed by the passion for black-and-white. The buildings on the right of Browns kicked it all off, and the revival spread like wildfire through Chester and then through England.

The Grosvenor Museum

Grosvenor Street; map C4

This newly refurbished museum charts the archaeology, natural history and local history of Chester and the area around. There are art and natural history galleries, but pride of place goes to the Roman tombstones, beautifully displayed in their own gallery. You will find quizzes and plenty of exciting hands-on activities for children.

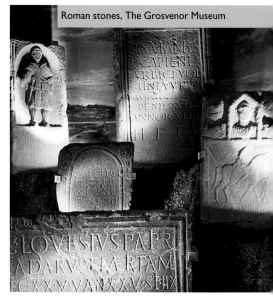
Roman stones, The Grosvenor Museum

At the back of the museum, linked by a conservatory, is No. 20 Castle Street, a splendid Georgian town house. Restored rooms and costumes show life in Chester over four centuries. If you want to know more about anything you've seen, browse through Cataline, the museum's computer catalogue, which has details of every arte-fact on the museum's three floors.

DON'T MISS

The Roman stones.
The Timeline Gallery, including a short video presentation showing how Chester has grown over the centuries – a very useful introduction to the city.
The Silver Gallery – a dazzling array of silver objects.
Open: daily; Mon–Sat 10.30–17.00, Sun 13.00–16.00

Georgian house, No. 20 Castle Street

Entry: free, but donations welcomed
Tel: 01244 402008/321616
Disabled access: limited
Other facilities: shop and tearoom

BILLY HOBBY'S WELL

I lov'd the tales that idle maids do tell,
Of wonders wrought at Billy Hobby's Well;
Where love-sick girls with leg immured would stand,
The right leg 'twas – the other on dry land,
With face so simple – stocking in the hand –
Wishing for husbands half a winter's day
With ninety times the zeal they used to pray.

Traditional Chester verse

Grosvenor Park

Grosvenor Park
Vicar's Lane; map E3

The land for Grosvenor Park was given to the city of Chester by the Marquess of Westminster in 1867. And what a gift it was! These lovely gardens occupy a large swathe of the slopes between the city (near Newgate) and the River Dee beyond the suspension bridge. Towards the river, shady paths wander through mossy stonework and greenery; the higher slopes are more open, with extensive lawns and flower beds shielded by trees from the streets beyond.

Like the riverside, the park has a festive atmosphere on a fine summer's day: the bedding plants are a picture and everywhere there's activity – families picnicking on the grass, office workers chatting as they enjoy lunch in the open air, pigeons looking for titbits, and squirrels darting in and out of the bushes.

The park has several exceptional features including a miniature railway, a scented garden for the blind and Billy Hobby's Well, said to be the home of a mischievous hobgoblin. In July the park is the focal point of the Chester Music Festival, with a big stage erected for the various bands (it's worth hanging around for a free concert).
Open: daily; summer: 8.30–dusk; winter: 8.30–15.30

The Nine Houses

The Nine Houses
Park Street; map D4

These six (yes, six!) charming almshouses
are perhaps best seen from the city walls
as you drop down towards the river
from Newgate. Unusually for Chester,
they date from around 1650. Equally
unusual is their timber-framed structure
on a sandstone base – rare elsewhere in
Britain. Fortunately, they were rescued
by the City Council from near derelic-
tion in 1969. The little plaque SMP and
SOP on the houses indicates the parish
boundary between St Michael's and
St Olave's churches.

River Dee

Chester's river is without doubt one of
its great treasures. It was the Dee that
attracted the Romans here in the first
place, both for its crossing place and its
potential as a port. On either side of
Chester, the Dee forms two long bends,

Fun on the Dee

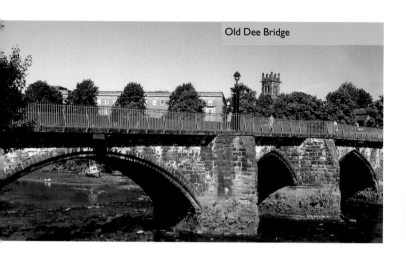

Old Dee Bridge

enclosing the racecourse at the western end and Earl's Eye meadows to the east. Between these, the river runs straight, with wooded banks on one side and the slopes of the city on the other. Since the estuary silted up centuries ago, the river hasn't been used by serious forms of transport. Instead it's a source of delight to thousands of locals and visitors. In summer the banks of the river are just a lovely place to be. Here beneath the trees people mess about in boats, eat and drink, listen to bands, play, or just sit and watch it all happen.

RIVER COURSE

Chester's racecourse was the site of the Roman harbour. The River Dee once ran beneath the city walls on the opposite side of The Roodee to its present course.

Bridges over the Dee

There are three fine bridges near the city. The oldest is Old Dee Bridge, near where the Romans first built a timber crossing. Old Dee Bridge dates from the 14th century, and was last widened in 1826. Nearby is the dramatic weir, first created in the 11th century to provide power for corn mills and fisheries upstream. Downstream, near the castle, is Grosvenor Bridge, built 1827–31, a graceful stone arch that was once the largest single-span arch in Europe. Upstream, by The Groves, is the Queen's Park suspension bridge, built in 1923 to replace a private bridge constructed in 1859 to link the posh new suburb of Queen's Park with the city.

Roman Amphitheatre

Little St John Street; map E3

Ironically, the Romans' largest construction, the amphitheatre, was found by accident only in 1929. It stood outside their fortress, to the south-east, its walls 10 metres (33 feet) high and 90 metres (100 yards) in diameter. Half of the arena has been revealed and a lot more, beneath more recent buildings, remains to be explored.

Records reveal that the amphitheatre was the largest of its type in Britain, seating around 7,000 people. It would be dramatic to say that they flocked here to witness bloodshed in grisly ways – gladiator contests, tussles with animals and executions, for instance. The truth is less exciting. The occasional gladiator may have put in an appearance, but most of the time the amphitheatre was used for weapons training and parades for the troops. There must have been an occasional execution, too, for near the north entrance was a shrine to Nemesis, the Roman god of retribution, a reminder to soldiers that the law was carried out by humans but dictated by divine order.

Open: daily; Easter–30 Sept
10.00–18.00; 1 Oct–Easter 10.00–13.00 and 14.00–16.00
Entry: free
Tel: 0161 242 1400
Disabled access: limited

Roman Garden
Newgate; map D4–E4
This lovely garden takes only about ten minutes to walk through; but you can sit here for as long as you like! It stretches in gentle layers from Newgate down to the banks of the River Dee. The idea, first conceived in 1949 and developed in recent years, was to create a setting that Chester's occupying Romans might have made and enjoyed. Real Roman columns from the bath house, previously hidden beneath the rubble of centuries, are now set among authentic, aromatic Italian trees and greenery.

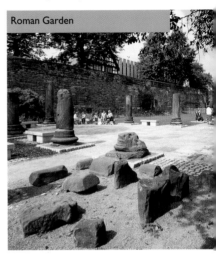
Roman Garden

The result, on a sunny summer's day, is a truly magical atmosphere, guaranteed to delight the senses. The sunlight plays on the columns and the scent from the herbal and medicinal shrubs wafts around. Adding a cosmopolitan touch is the excited chatter of numerous languages, for the garden is very popular with the many overseas students who come to Chester to study English. The shape of the paths reflects a serpent coiled round a rod – the emblem of the Roman god of medicine, Aesculapius.

Open: 24 hours a day, 365 days a year
Entry: free

The Roodee (Chester Racecourse)
Map A4–A6

The name of The Roodee, the 'soup-bowl' of land that forms Chester's race-course, means 'island of the cross'. And it *was* an island, or at least a partial one, for the river once swept in a curve round its eastern side, beneath the city walls. Here against those walls the Romans built their port. A medieval cross still stands alone in the middle of the course. This is one of the oldest racecourses in Britain, and it originated like this. The men and boys of the town used to divide into teams each Shrove Tuesday for a mad game based on getting a football from The Roodee to the 'common hall' (town hall). However, things got violent, so in 1541 Henry Gee, the Mayor, cancelled the game and instead put up a cup for a horse race and an archery contest.

Races take place here throughout the summer, the May Festival being the biggest. Chester Races is special for its electric atmosphere, generated by the small size and tightness of the course and the cockpit-like set-up. You don't even need binoculars to see how your horse is running. There's more about the races on page 84.

Open: races held May–Sept
Entry: varies – phone for details
Tel: 01244 304600
Website:
www.chester-races.co.uk
Disabled access: disabled racegoers each with one companion may enter restricted areas free of charge. Passes issued from the marquee

The Roodee

The Rows
Map C3–D3

If you had to choose one feature which distinguishes Chester from any other city in the world, it is the Rows – historic galleried walkways above the streets, fronting a rich array of distinctive shops, cafés and boutiques. Higher still are black-and-white half-timbered gable ends, the look characteristic of medieval English architecture in the north-west of England.

The Rows

Origin of the Rows

The Rows get their name from the traders who carried on their businesses here: Shoemakers' Row, Cookes' Row and Ironmongers' Row being examples. The mercers of Mercers' Row were textile dealers, while Lorimers, as in Lorimers' Row, made harnesses for horses. Welsh Row wasn't packed with Welshmen – they just sold Welsh flannel there! Although today the Rows are exclusively commercial, in the Middle Ages shopkeepers lived on the premises. A merchant's home consisted of a living hall and a shop over a stone cellar (which was necessary for security). As the sandstone bedrock was only just below the surface, cellars had to be virtually at street level. All other accommodation was therefore pushed upwards. From the early 16th century, shops expanded outwards too, supported on posts set in the street. In time, more shops filled the spaces at street level. Over the centuries the gaps between the houses were built up and the galleries joined together.

Later changes

In the Civil War (1644–46) Chester took a huge pounding from the guns of Oliver Cromwell's army, who laid siege to the city for 18 months. The result was widespread dilapidation, which was only slowly repaired by succeeding generations. The Georgians enclosed the Rows, adding new brick façades. The Victorians looked back to the Middle Ages, copying the half-timbered appearance that gives Chester its identity today.

Layers of history

Along the Rows and in the shops you'll find fascinating glimpses of the layers of history: the sloping outerboards in the galleries, once used for displaying wares; the rough wattle and daub walls of the Middle Ages; the arched cellars below;

deeper still, very occasional bits of Roman architecture.

DON'T MISS

The wattle and daub walls exposed at the Boot Inn, Eastgate Street.
The arched cellar underneath Bookland on Bridge Street.
The Roman hypocaust (heating system) at the back of the restaurant Spud-u-Like in Bridge Street.
God's Providence House.
The medieval house revealed upstairs in The Rather Nice Card Shop in Bridge Street.

Shropshire Union Canal
Map A1–E1

The River Dee isn't the only waterway in Chester. The city's stretch of the

GODS PROVIDENCE IS MINE INHERITANCE

GOD'S PROVIDENCE

God's Providence House in Watergate Street was originally built in 1652, four years after a plague which killed 2,000 Chester inhabitants in 10 months.
The motto on its frontage, 'God's providence is mine inheritance', is an expression of thanks that none of the family died during the epidemic.

Shropshire Union Canal passes only 5 minutes' walk away from the Town Hall and, what's more, it's a section that's full of interest, with a deep cutting, several locks and an attractive wharf and basin. Although many canals were superseded by the railways in the early 19th century, they have gained a new lease of life in the last 30 years as a leisure facility. In Chester, holiday narrowboats make a regular and colourful sight in summer.

Don't think you have to go boating to enjoy canal life. For one thing, the towpaths built for plodding barge horses now make excellent gentle footpaths and cycleways. For another, there are few more relaxing ways to spend time than sitting beside locks watching boaters go up or down. If a canal walk appeals to you, try the one on pages 24–25. Alternatively, if you just want to sit and watch things happen, a good place to go is Telford's Warehouse (see page 80) for a coffee or a snack.

Stanley Palace
Watergate Street; map B3

If you want to see what a real Tudor mansion looks like, this fine house is only ten minutes on foot from the Town Hall. Built during the reign of Elizabeth I and later owned by the Stanley family, the Earls of Derby, it has the wonderful black-and-white look echoed elsewhere in the city. Although the shape and the surroundings have changed over time, you have only to walk inside to roll back 400 years. Everywhere the polished oak of the panelling and floors greets you.

DON'T MISS

The section of wall which reveals the ancient wattle and daub.
The 'screen' upstairs where you can see the original timber-peg construction.

The Stanley crest

The plaster ceiling in the Queen Anne room. The curved beam over the hall fireplace. This was taken from a ship broken up centuries ago in the nearby port area. The baby in the basket in the crest in the window on the stairs (see opposite). You'll have to look hard – it's incredibly tiny!

The baby in the basket

There is more than one legend about the baby and its basket in the Stanley crest. Some say it derives from an ancestral knight of the Stanleys, away for some years on a crusade to the Holy Land. His wife played the field while he was away and was nursing a baby when he returned. Her story was that a griffin had left the baby in a basket. We're not told if he believed her! The alternative version is that Sir Thomas Latham, a Stanley ancestor, had no son by his wife but one by his mistress. To get the child accepted as heir, Sir Tom had it placed in an eagle's nest where he and his wife just happened to find it! The ruse is said to have worked.

Open: most days of the week, but ring to check
Tel: 01244 325586
Disabled access: limited

Stanley Palace

HIDDEN CHESTER

Chester's rich heritage means that many treasures are tucked away in unlikely places. Here's where to find some of them.

Roman strongroom
The *sacellum* which housed the 20th Legion's standards is in Hamilton Place, very near the Town Hall. Turn right down the alley by the Dublin Packet Inn in Northgate Street and look on your right.

Roman hypocaust
The Roman bath house, with its hot and cold rooms, was where soldiers came to chill out, literally. Its heating system is in the cellar at the back of Spud-u-Like in Bridge Street (map C3). Just ask to see it.

Roman wall
Part of the original Roman fortress wall lies below the present city wall just outside Kaleyards Gate (map D2).

Boot Inn

Tudor house

The Rather Nice Card Shop

Bookland

and cow dung). The Boot Inn, Eastgate Street (map D3), has left a section exposed for viewing.

A Tudor house
No. I White Friars, just off Bridge Street (map C4), is a superb Tudor house with jettying (protruding upper floor) and galleried windows.

A 1659 rectory
Upstairs in The Rather Nice Card Shop, Bridge Street (map C3), you'll see the rear of the original old St Michael's Rectory, with its stone corbels and lovely woodcarving.

St Werburgh
The head of Chester's Saxon patron saint is depicted in the ancient abbey gateway off Northgate Street, opposite the Town Hall. St Werburgh's head is the farthest of the three stone roof bosses.

13th-century crypts
Chester's Rows are built upon vaulted stone cellars. One, built 1270–80, is now the rear part of Bookland, Bridge Street (map C3). Another is Watergates Wine Bar (see page 76).

A 15th-century hall
Leche House (Sofa Workshop) in Watergate Street (map C3) was once a medieval hall. Go in and try to spot where Catholic priests once hid. (See also 18th-century vandalism below.)

Medieval walls
House walls were once made of wattle (interwoven branches) and daub (mud

18th-century vandalism
On the first-floor front window of Leche House (Sofa Workshop) in Watergate Street, the famous lexicographer and wit Dr Samuel Johnson scratched a lady's name and a date. Have a look and see if you can find it.

Chester's Victorian market
We can still see a small sample of the 19th-century market façade, demolished in the 1960s to give way to the Forum Shopping Centre (map C2). Facing the Dublin Packet Inn in Northgate Street, look to your right.

A crop of snails
Many craftsmen have their own trademark. On the Town Hall gates in Northgate Street (map C2), made in 1992, three tiny snails are hiding, one on the right-hand gate, another in the central gate and one that's etched so small don't even think of looking for it!

BREATHING SPACE

Chester is famous for the vibrancy of its street life, especially in summer. But the odds are that, at some point in the day, you'll want to take a breather from it all. The good news is that there are many spots to spend a quiet few minutes. Here are some suggestions, starting from the centre of the city.

Chester Cathedral;
map C2
Churches used to be places of sanctuary and Chester Cathedral still is, not least of all on a hot day. If you want to stay outside, head for Cathedral Green – that's the area on the south (city centre) side by the bell tower. The Cheshire Regiment's Garden of Remembrance is here and it is a lovely place to sit and enjoy the sun. Don't be tempted to feed the squirrels, though – they can become nasty. If you've had enough sun, go inside the cathedral and sit in the cool of the nave.

The bell tower

Either that or enjoy the cloister garden with Stephen Broadbent's statue, *The Water of Life*. Or you could head for the refectory for coffee or lunch. It's lofty and restful.

Roman Garden;
map D4–E4
The Roman Garden (see page 44) meanders down to the river from Newgate, and is a superb spot to spend a quiet few minutes amid the ancient columns, enjoying the smell of fragrant Italian herbal plants.

Grosvenor Park;
map E3
A little further on is Grosvenor Park, a delightful place to sit, enjoy the wonderful flowers and simply watch life go on around you.

River Dee
Beyond the Roman Garden and Grosvenor Park is Chester's other chief place of retreat, the river. Wander down to The Groves to feed the swans and watch the boaters. There's always something going on here. If you fancy

combining that with a coffee or a drink, stroll a few yards upstream to the Blue Moon Café or the Boathouse pub. Or, of course, you could always have your drink on board, during a half-hour river cruise (see page 83).

For the energetic
If you are not tired but just want some peace and quiet, how about taking a walk on the city walls or join the canal towpath at Frodsham Street (map D1) for a cool stroll through the cutting?

LISTEN TO THE BAND
At weekends in summer, bands play in the bandstand at the river's edge in The Groves (map D5–E4). There are plenty of seats and you couldn't have a finer setting in which to sit, soak up the sun and savour the sound.

SHOPPING

counter c

As well as its lovely river, superb city walls and a splendid cathedral, what draws many people to Chester is the shopping. Chester's two-tier central streets are a shopper's paradise. This section gives you a street-by-street rundown, and a selection of different kinds of shops.

Counter Culture (page 67)

Opening hours

Most shops open seven days a week, even during the winter. On Sundays, though, opening hours are usually shorter.

SHOPPING BY AREA

Watergate Street; map B3–C3

A good place to start. This street has shopping at two levels, and is one of the best areas in Chester for varied and unusual shops. The street has antiques, jewellery, designer clothes, traditionally-made goods, unusual gifts plus two excellent children's shops (toys and more).

Northgate Street; map C1–C3

Mainly high-street names at the Town Hall end with, further up, odd flashes of inspiration. Look out for The Hat Company, The Bridal House and, in a different vein, The Cheese Shop. Rufus Court (see below) is off Northgate Street near the arch at the top end.

Chester Market; map C2

A large, traditional market with an authentic markety smell, situated just behind the Town Hall. Dozens of stalls sell all sorts of stuff, including fresh fruit and vegetables, fish, wool, knick-knacks, clothes, meat, haberdashery, crafts, old medals, badges and uniforms amongst much more. You'll pay less here than you will elsewhere.

Rufus Court, off Northgate Street; map C1

This is a fairly new court-yard development, but quaint for all that. It has an eclectic mix of small shops selling, amongst other things, abstract art, violins, postcards, stamps and furnishings, plus there are various kinds of eateries.

OYEZ! OYEZ!
Don't miss one of Chester's unique and enjoyable free treats (midday Tue–Sat, May–Aug) when the city's Town Crier delivers his (or her!) proclama-tions from the Cross in Eastgate Street (map C3). Lots of banter with the audience.

Bridge Street; map C3

Another good street for individual shops, especially up in the Rows. Potential purchases include cook-ware, designer menswear, children's boutiques, tradi-tional goods, green men and gargoyles.

Eastgate Street; map D3

Mostly high-street names here, but there's a sparkling array of jewellers' shops on the city side of the arch.

Foregate Street; map E2

Mainly high-street names.

Out of town

Cheshire Oaks, Ellesmere, Europe's largest outlet centre, only 6 miles north of Chester. More than 140 stores selling most big-name designer labels. Tel: 0151 348 5600

SELECTED SHOPS

High-street shops

Eastgate is where you will find most of the big names. Linking Eastgate and Bridge Street (in a dogleg sort of way) is the Grosvenor Centre (map D3), where you'll find shops with familiar names.

Antiques

Without doubt, Watergate Street (map C3) is your best bet. Cestrian Antiques has two very attractive shops next door to each other, and there are others, too. If you're really hunting in earnest for a bargain, try Boughton, a suburb east of the city centre. It has quite a few shops worth rummaging through.

Art galleries

You'll find several galleries in Watergate Street (map C3). Elsewhere The Arc, just off Bridge Street in Commonhall Street (map C3), has an elegant selection of primarily British arts and crafts. If your tastes veer towards the abstract, try Ascent in Rufus Court (map C1).

Clothes

Chester has many excellent clothes shops for men and women. If you start at the Cross (map C3) and go 100 metres (about 100 yards) east, west or south, you'll find most of them.

Cestrian Antiques

TREAT YOURSELF Remember humbugs, lemon sherbets, liquorice root? Drop into the Old Sweet Shop which is in St Werburgh Street for old-fashioned sweets.

Old Sweet Shop

Bridal wear
Northgate Street;
map C2
The Bridal House is the
place to go for everything
you need for brides and
bridesmaids, too.

Designer clothes
Lisa and Tessuti in
Watergate Street (map
C3) sell designer women's
wear, while Jade on
Eastgate Street (map D3)
is even more exclusive.

Pure on St Werburgh's
Street (map D2) has
designer fashion for
women of almost all ages
on three dazzling levels.

Hats
Northgate Street;
map C2
The Hat Company sells
hats for all occasions in
many colours and styles.

The Bridal House

Tessuti

Lisa

The Hat Company

Pure

Men's designer clothes

Tessuti in Watergate Street (map C3) also has a trendy man's shop. Marc and City Gate in Bridge Street (map C3) are also worth a visit. If you're looking for younger styles, St Werburgh Street (map C2–D2) is probably the best place to start.

Tessuti

Food

Northgate Street; map C1

C.S. Austin is a traditional butcher who sells a fantastically wide range of meats including kangaroo and crocodile! How about some wild boar and venison sausages?

The Cheese Shop has a huge range of cheeses for any palate, with local flavours a speciality. Their

C.S. Austin

Cheshire cheese actually comes from Cheshire. You should try it.

The Granary stocks a good selection of health foods.

Gifts

Bridge Street; map C3

Armadillo is an unusual shop selling gargoyles and green men.

Room has a range of gifts and furniture made from natural materials.

Godstall Lane, off St Werburgh Street; map D2

Go to Halcyon Days for that extra special gift: hand-painted enamel boxes and clocks, porcelain and bonbonnières.

Watergate Street; map C3

Batavia has unusual gifts, as well as furniture.

Harriet and Dee is a design-led gift shop whose stock includes unusual gadgets and lovely handmade cards.

Rainforest sells a range of eco-friendly and fair-trade items, including jewellery, clothes and world music.

The Cheese Shop

Uri Jacobi (page 64)

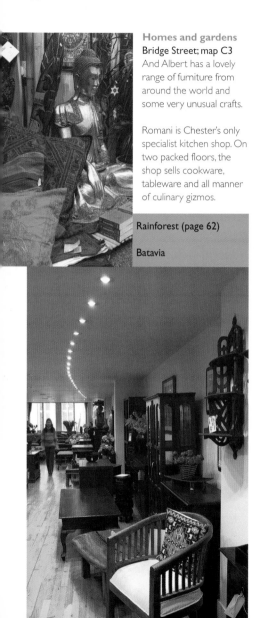

Homes and gardens

Bridge Street; map C3
And Albert has a lovely range of furniture from around the world and some very unusual crafts.

Romani is Chester's only specialist kitchen shop. On two packed floors, the shop sells cookware, tableware and all manner of culinary gizmos.

Rainforest (page 62)

Batavia

Room has all sorts of traditional goods, including furniture, candlesticks and gifts. It's a wee bit different.

Foregate Street; map E2
Lee Louise is a new-age shop with a good range of gifts, clothes, furniture and jewellery.

Pepper Street; map D4
This street has a proliferation of shops selling furnishings of all kinds.

Rufus Court; map C1
Afrasia specializes in African crafts and curios, while Nichols is worth looking at for furnishings.

Watergate Street; map C3
Don't miss Batavia and Sofa Workshop, or Uri Jacobi, which has a rich selection of oriental rugs and carpets.

Romani

Jewellery

Jewellery is one of Chester's specialities. Without doubt, Boodle and Dunthorne's, near the Eastgate Arch (map D3), is top of the tree – elegant and exclusive. But if your piggy bank won't stretch quite that far, don't despair, for within a stone's throw of B&D's there are many excellent jewellers, which include:

Bridge Street; map C3

Lowe and Sons who have superb silver.

Lowe and Sons

Sofa Workshop

AFTER A LONG DAY ...

How about some holistic aromatherapy for sore shoulders and tired feet? At The Scented Garden, Godstall Lane (map D2), Laura and her team will give you a delicious neck and back massage, or some reflexology and a pedicure. Treatments last 35–90 minutes. Or you could indulge in the full package (facial, neck and back massage, and manicure). Tel: 01244 344335 for details.

Penhaligons, Eastgate Street

Daisy and Tom

Leather goods
Bridge Street; map C3
Shuttleworth's specializes in good-quality leather goods from purses and wallets to handbags and briefcases. They also have a large luggage department with suitcases of all sizes (to take home all that shopping!).

Toys
Watergate Street; map C3
Daisy and Tom is a large and colourful store featuring everything to do with children – upmarket toys, books, clothes … you name it.

Toycraft in the same street is an established and traditional toy shop.

Other specialist shops
Bridge Street; map C3
If you visit The Rather Nice Card Shop, do make sure you go upstairs, where, as well as Kites Aloft (another specialist retailer), you'll find delightful historical features (see page 53).

Eastgate Street; map D3
Counter Culture carries a full range of modern designer jewellery.

The Cross; map C3
Walton's specializes in watches and diamonds.

Further afield, try Bizarre in Rufus Court (map C1) for trendy jewellery and Rainforest in Watergate Street (map C3) for traditional designs.

Daisy and Tom

You certainly won't go hungry on your visit to Chester. Apart from the usual chains, there are some terrific, independently-owned places to lunch, to dine, or snack out in between! On the next few pages are details of those with a reputation for great food.

If you've got a particular style of cuisine in mind, then look at the list below. If you're open to ideas, then one way to decide where to eat is to head for one of Chester's restaurant quarters and browse through the window menus. Good places to start are Cuppin Street, St Werburgh Street and Northgate Street.

EATING AND DRINKING

Alfresco

CAFES

Alfresco
St Werburgh Street;
map D2
You are sure to be tempted by the ciabatta fillings – try the Italian chicken or duck, the pavlovas and other meringues. Almost everything here is made on the premises and the prices are reasonable. You don't have to eat in. Many locals take their food away and enjoy a picnic in the nearby Cathedral Green.

Blue Moon Café
The Groves; map E4

You'll love the Blue Moon, a retro riverside coffee bar which takes its theme from the 50s and early 60s. Nostalgic pictures on the walls and a 1961 juke-box. Good cappuccino, soup and specials, all-day breakfasts, snacks, home-made cakes – no wonder locals rave about it. You can sit outside, too.

Chester Cathedral Refectory
Abbey Square; map C2

Just because it's in the 13th-century monks' hall doesn't mean you'll go hungry here. It's easily reached from the street, and for a very reasonable price they serve good-value, home-cooked, hearty meals, such as cottage pie, lasagne, and jacket potatoes. Morning

coffee and afternoon tea, you'll find soups, jacket potatoes, light lunches and puddings. Two bonuses here – you can sit outside and it's very child friendly, with baby changing facilities on hand.

Deecafe.com
Lower Bridge Street; map D5

The only internet café in central Chester, a bijou place nestling in the shadow of the walls next to Old Dee Bridge. You can enjoy teas, coffees or light meals while you surf.

Blue Moon Café

Deecafe.com

HAVE A PAV
For fantastic pavlovas Alfresco in St Werburgh Street is unbeat-able. Drool at them through the window before you buy.

coffee and afternoon tea are also available.

Chester Rows Café
Chester Visitor Centre, Vicar's Lane; map E3

This unpretentious café sells simple, wholesome food at very reasonable prices. As well as morning

Gabby's Crêperie
Music Hall Passage; map C2

If you didn't know about Gabby's, you wouldn't notice it. This tiny kiosk, tucked away in an alley between Northgate Street and the cathedral, produces – while you

Chez Jules

watch – superb crêpes with delicious fillings. If you are in a savoury mood, try the chargrilled veggies and cheese; if you feel like something sweet, how about a Black Forest crêpe with cherries, chocolate drops, cream and brandy?

Hattie's
Rufus Court; map C1
By day, Rufus Court is a peaceful corner of a busy city. This old-fashioned, cosy teashop is worth the 5-minute walk past the Town Hall and up towards the arch at the top of Northgate Street.

Katie's
Watergate Street; map C3
An old-fashioned teashop, centrally located, in a 14th-century building.

Weinholt's
Northgate Street; map C3
A coffee lounge that specializes in pâtisseries and pies, which you can also buy to take away. Try a steak pie or, if you are looking for something sweet, a fudge doughnut.

RESTAURANTS
Brasseries
Brasserie
10/16 Brookdale Place
Cheshire Life magazine voted this Best New Restaurant of 2002. Its popularity with the wealthier end of the market certainly backs this up and you may well need to book ahead. The cooking is British with Mediterranean influences.
Tel: 01244 322288

Chez Jules
Northgate Street; map C1
You are sure to love this simply-furnished, two-floor bistro with a terrific local following. The friendly staff serve a range of French dishes with an English touch. Expect food cooked with garlic, cream and rich sauces. Lunch is popular, but the atmosphere in the evenings is amazing, especially on Tuesdays when everyone can enjoy a free bottle of wine with their meal.
Tel: 01244 400014

Franc's
Cuppin Street; map C4
An old favourite with Chester residents, Franc's is very French, with intimate, candlelit tables even

at lunchtime. Two of its three floors are art nouveau and dark oak in style; the top floor has a lovely medieval roof. The best thing about Franc's, though, is the food, and there are many good-value deals at various times of the day and night. At lunch (which continues until 17.00) you can have three courses for as little as £7.
Tel: 01244 317952

La Brasserie
The Chester Grosvenor, Eastgate Street; map D3
One of three eating venues within the Grosvenor's lush portals, this is an informal Parisian-style place with wooden floors, marble tables and scrolly chairs, open all day and evening. Expect to pay at least £20 for a two-course table d'hôte lunch, but the high standards justify the prices.
Tel: 01244 324024

Moules à Go-Go
Watergate Street; map C3
A popular, modern, friendly brasserie serving Franco-Belgian specialities, such as moules frites, steak frites, frites and mayo, rotisserie chicken frites. Get the idea?
Tel: 01244 348818

British
The Arkle
The Chester Grosvenor, Eastgate Street; map D3
The Arkle represents the high point of eating in Chester: the elegant, traditional dining room of the hotel serves cuisine that has won – and held on to – a Michelin star. The menu changes seasonally with the accent on using fresh food that is grown locally and cooked in an imaginative way. There's a vast wine cellar too. Don't forget that the dress code is jacket and tie, please.
Tel: 01244 324024

The Blue Bell Restaurant
Northgate Street; map C1
Occupying what is probably the oldest domestic building in Chester, The Blue Bell is one of Chester's flagship restaurants. It has an intimate, comfortable atmosphere, and is simply but elegantly furnished. The owner takes a great pride in the standard of her food.
Tel: 01244 317758

La Brasserie

The Blue Bell

Pastarazzi Ristorante

Olive Tree Restaurant
Green Bough Hotel,
Hoole Road

One of Chester's major food surprises. Owners Philip and Janice Martin (Philip trained at London's Savoy Hotel) aim to provide fine dining without the stuffiness, at an affordable price. The cuisine is British with a French touch, the accent firmly placed on flavour. The Olive Tree has received rave reviews in several publications.
Tel: 01244 326241

Chinese
Shang Hai
Hoole Road

Excellent food in a modern, sophisticated setting on two floors. A little more expensive than the average Chinese restaurant, but worth it!
Tel: 01244 323888

Slow Boat
Frodsham Street; map D1

This large upstairs restaurant overlooking the canal serves excellent value-for-money food and is very popular. It's worth checking out their special offers, particularly if you've got several mouths to feed.
Tel: 01244 317873

Indian
Shere Khan
Pepper Street; map D4

You won't miss Shere Khan with its plate-glass windows and the warm, exciting colours of the walls. The food is unusual, too, but very tasty.
Tel: 01244 342349

Italian
Pastarazzi Ristorante
29 Grosvenor Street;
map C4

Pastarazzi is Chester's leading Italian restaurant, plushly set in a grand Victorian room, and serving a broad menu of freshly-cooked food. It's not the cheapest place in town but 60,000 customers happily eat here every year.
Tel: 01244 400029

Pizza Express
52–54 Lower Bridge
Street; map D4

Chain restaurant, excellent for families, in one of Chester's most spectacular buildings.
Tel: 01244 350625

Vito's Trattoria
25 Lower Bridge Street;
map D4

Great fresh food in an informal bistro atmos-phere. Prompt service and reasonable prices.
Tel: 01244 317330

Japanese
Samsi Yakitori
Watergate Street;
map B3

This highly praised restaurant delivers all that its exotic decor promises. Its authentic cuisine includes influences from many parts of Japan. Fish dishes include Black Tiger Prawn tempura; meat dishes include rib-eye steak sukiyaki which is cooked at the table.
Tel: 01244 344883

Mediterranean
Ego
14 Grosvenor Street;
map C4

The tables are plain, the chairs have straw seats and the food is good. The buzzword is fusion cooking: translated, this means new and exotic ingredients added to traditional dishes. In this case, pasta, chicken, duck and fish are cooked in a variety of Mediterranean styles. As with its sister restaurant, Chez Jules, many Chester people come here again and again.
Tel: 01244 346512

La Tasca

Mexican
Dos Americas
43 Watergate Row; map C3

This Tex-Mex restaurant has a good reputation as a fun, lively place serving good food. The decor is warm and welcoming and the staff friendly. Particularly popular is the early evening 'Beat the clock': if you order a two-course meal at 6.10 p.m. you pay £6.10, at 6.15 p.m. you pay £6.15, and so on. Whatever the time of day, however, you'll get good value food here.
Tel: 01244 347207

Ruan Orchid

Spanish
La Tasca
6–10 Cuppin Street; map C4

Dark wood, bare boards, candles in bottles, tiled dado – after a glass or two of Rioja you'll swear you're back on holiday on the Costa del Sol! Many locals remember enjoyable nights spent in this lively, atmospheric place.
Tel: 01244 400887

Thai
Ruan Orchid
14 Lower Bridge Street; map D4

It's not hard to see why people come back to this long-established restaurant. Medieval stone walls are cleverly given a warm inviting feel with exotic greenery and attractive Thai hangings. Specialities include the Ruan Orchid starter (five delicious starters in one), Crying Tiger (sirloin steak with a hot dip), and colourful curries, such as chicken red and king prawn green.
Tel: 01244 400661

WINE BARS
Bar Lounge
Watergate Street; map C3

This place was transformed from a traditional pub into Chester's most popular cocktail venue, with squishy sofas inside and a large terrace outside. The food goes down well with the locals, too. Watch out on race days – it gets very packed.

Dutton's
Godstall Lane; map D2

Chester people love to lunch at Dutton's, a bustling eatery hiding modestly in a tiny alley near the cathedral. Although they serve evening meals, the place is busiest between 12.00 and 14.00, and you may have time for a drink while you wait for a table. The staff are cheery, speedy and attentive. The food – from brunches, via wraps to larger meals – is adventurous, well presented and excellent value.

Tonic (page 76)

TREAT YOURSELF
The Library of the Chester Grosvenor is the elegant lounge where you can have anything from cups of tea to champagne cocktails. Why not treat yourself to afternoon tea? You'll pay about £15 but it's a memorable experience – finger sandwiches, buttered scones, clotted cream and jam, home-made French pastries. Do ask for a take-home bag for anything you can't eat – you won't get any funny looks.

The Library, Chester Grosvenor

Loaf
Music Hall Passage; map C2

This ultra-smooth, slinkily-lit, late venue bar is open till two in the morning. One of the places to be seen in Chester, it has two simple menus: from lunch till 19.00 they offer a range of sandwiches, salads, wraps and chunky mains; from 19.00 till late it's tasty dips to enjoy with your wine or cocktail.

Tonic
Rufus Court; map C1

This ritzy café-bar is tucked away near Northgate, but well worth finding – as long as you're not on too tight a budget. The decor is modern, simple and elegant; the food is fresh, home-made traditional with a twist,

while the customers are mostly aged 30+.

Watergates Wine Bar
Watergate Street; map C3

This unique wine bar occupies Chester's finest vaulted cellar, with various other comfy catacombs branching off. It's popular and highly atmospheric.

PUBS

Of Chester's historic inns, The Falcon in Bridge Street (map C4), the back room of the Boot Inn in Eastgate Street (map D3), and The Pied Bull in Northgate Street (map C1) are the most ancient, yet typical, examples of English locals. The Albion in Park Street (map D4) is a unique throwback to the First World War era (see

pages 78–79). The Albion also provides hearty, wholesome British fare and The Pied Bull offers reliable pub grub.

The Falcon

A PINT TO BOOT

Raise your glass to Samuel Smith. This long-established Yorkshire brewer is committed to excellent beer at low prices. The historic, 'spit and sawdust' Boot Inn at Rows level on Eastgate Street is where you'll find it. Go into the back room, the ancient part of the pub with an old range fireplace.

The Pied Bull

THE ALBION INN

The Albion Inn is a true gem, hidden below the city walls at the corner of Park Street and Albion Street (map D4), a neat *Coronation-Street*-style terrace just down from Newgate. The Albion has been voted one of Britain's top city pubs; it is very British, very different, and very special.

Its whole style is that of an English public house at the time of the 1914–18 war. The decor is William Morris, adorned by many fascinating old posters and signs. Real coal fires burn in winter. The drinks are traditional, mainly hand-pulled bitter and single malt whisky. Don't come here for alcopops! And don't even think of calling it a theme pub, or there's no knowing how Mike Mercer, landlord for over 30 years, would react.

Mr Mercer describes his popular food as 'what your mother would like you to eat' – hearty portions of traditional British fare, using the best produce that he can muster. Expect local sausages, oatcakes from Staffordshire, liver and bacon and other old-time favourites.

Conversation thrives at The Albion, as there is no music to interfere (apart from an occasional round-the-piano sing-song). Although no under-18s are admitted, it's certainly

The Albion Inn

The Albion Inn

not a haven for old fogeys, just a wide age range of satisfied customers.

Before you go dashing off there, a few words of warning. Mr Mercer has strong ideas of what a pub should be. His philosophy is that if you don't like it, there are many more who do. Firstly, the things you *won't* find here. The sign outside reads:

'No chips
No fry-ups
No UHT
No silly foil portions
No children
No plastic oak trees.'

Secondly, Mr Mercer is discriminating about his customers. We've already told you about the under-18s, but the selectivity doesn't stop there. There's no welcome for over-loud folk, or anybody who's had too much to drink. That's why the front door stays closed during the races.

So if, after reading this, you choose to visit The Albion (and we hope you do), go quietly through its doors, resolved to enjoy its special atmosphere by blending in. You won't find many places like it.

AN EVENING OUT

Chester offers many opportunities to have a great night out. Restaurants are covered on pages 70–76, so here are a few other suggestions.

Loaf

Dining cruises

L'Eau T'Cuisine, the Mill Hotel's restaurant-boat, offers romantic evening dining cruises on the canal. Locals enjoy them too.
Tel: 01244 350035

Bithell Boats

Barbecue cruises on long, summer weekend evenings 19.30–late. Booking essential for both these dining cruises.
Tel: 01244 325394

Ghost Walks

Ghost Hunter Tours start from the Town Hall on summer evenings, Thursday to Saturday.
Tel: 01244 402445

Cinema

The Odeon in Northgate Street (map C2) is a high-quality multi-screen cinema that you don't need a car to get to.
Information line:
0870 505 0007

Theatre

The Gateway Theatre in Hamilton Place (map C3) has a wide range of home-produced and touring shows spanning drama, stand-up comedy, opera, music and dance. Worth checking what's on before you arrive.

Tel: 01244 340392
Website: www.
chestergateway.co.uk

Music

Telford's Warehouse, Tower Wharf; map A1
A comfortable and atmospheric canalside music venue (mainly blues and rock). Provides international cuisine. For the over 21s only.
Tel: 01244 390090

Alexander's Bar

Old Harkers Arms, Russell Street
Popular, smart, relaxed canalside bar. Food, wine and real ale.

Room, Watergate Street; map C3
Very trendy and a popular venue with the city's young people.

Alexander's Bar, Rufus Court; map C1
The programme – acoustic, jazz, blues, dance, comedy – varies daily (except Mondays) and is often free. Book to eat here and you're guaranteed a table for the music. Tel: 01244 340005

Classical concerts
Take place regularly in Chester Cathedral and the Town Hall. Details from the Tourist Information Centre.

Laser Quest
Volunteer Street; map D4
Zap your friends in the sci-fi battlezone of the future – if you dare! Tel: 01244 400500

Bars and pubs
As well as the bars and pubs listed on pages 74 and 76, you may enjoy:

Club Globe, Steam Mill Street
Relaxing place by the canal for 30+ clientele to drink and/or eat.

CHESTER MYSTERY PLAYS
This ancient cycle of medieval religious drama takes place every five years at the beginning of July; in this decade 2003 and 2008. Tel: 01244 313400

Night clubs
Loaf, Music Hall Passage; map C2
Cool and youngish. Drinks and nibbles until 2.00 (see page 76). Tel: 01244 354041

Brannigan's, Love Street; map E2
Mixed clientele, live music (often tribute bands). Tel: 01244 319913

Laser Quest

TOURS AND TRIPS

Chester is a fascinating city with a rich history. This section tells you about some of the excellent trips and tours on offer to help you explore it.

On foot

Chester is best seen on foot. The central streets are free of traffic for most of the day, and there are city walls, the river and canalside paths to explore. Remember to pack a pair of comfortable shoes. The city centre is compact and you may just want to wander around. On the other hand, guides make sure you don't miss any hidden gems. Excellent professional guides lead walks from the Visitor Centre (map E3) and the Town Hall (map C2) twice a day in the summer, mornings only in winter. If you fancy something more memorable, a fully-kitted Roman soldier will take you round on certain days in summer. More details about guided walks on pages 28–29.

Roman soldier guide

If you are interested in spooks, there are summer evening Ghost Hunter Tours (see page 80).

By bus

A good way to get your bearings is to hop on one of the City Transport open-topped sightseeing buses which cruise around the city in summer. As you go, a guide gives you the lowdown on what you're seeing. The full tour takes an hour and includes the railway station, but you can jump on or off at several points around the city. Tickets cost about £7 – less for concessions. If you're going to take a river tour as well (see below), buy a combined ticket for less than £10 and save some money.
Tel: 01244 347457.

On the water

A cruise on the River Dee is a must. Every day in summer, weekends only in winter, three-decker showboats do half-hour cruises (price around £5 for adults), which you can combine with a city bus tour. For a few pounds more, there is a two-hour Ironbridge cruise into the country near Eaton Hall.

Ghost Hunter Tours

On all trips, you can drink tea, coffee or something stronger. For more info, contact Bithell Boats.
Tel: 01244 325394
Website: www. showboatsofchester.co.uk

If you want to eat as you sail, then the Mill Hotel

does regular gourmet canal cruises, lunchtime and evening, in their restaurant cruiser, *L'Eau T'Cuisine*. A romantic dining experience; advance booking essential.
Tel: 01244 350035
Website: www.millhotel.com

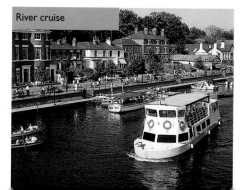
River cruise

WHAT'S ON

When it comes to events, Chester is quiet in January and February, busier in spring, and hectic from May through to Christmas. These are the highlights:

Late February–March
Chester Food and Drink Festival
A week of tastings, markets and special promotions in the city's fine eateries.
Tel: 01244 402330

March
Chester Folk Day
A taster for the main folk festival in May.
Tel: 01352 762931

A FREE VIEW OF THE RACES
You don't have to pay to go to the races! For a free view of the action, the place to go is Nuns Road (map B4). The prime position is between side-streets Greyfriars and Blackfriars. Don't expect to be there alone though!

Motor Racing at Oulton Park, Tarporley
The season starts in March and lasts until October.
Tel: 01829 760301

Cheshire and Warrington Science Festival
Science in a fun and interesting way. Guest speakers, hands-on stuff, celebrities, lots for children.
Tel: 01244 375444

May
Chester Races
Races are held May–Sept (see page 45). The May Festival is the biggest meeting of the year.
Tel: 01244 304600

Folk Festival
A weeekend of ceilidhs, concerts, dance and crafts.
Tel: 01352 762931

June
The Lord Mayor's Show and Chester Carnival
Weekend of parades, sideshows and so on, in the city centre and on The Roodee, too.
Tel: 01244 402126 (Lord Mayor's Show)

Midsummer Watch Parade

Midsummer Watch Parades
Unique cavalcade of curious medieval characters.
Tel: 01244 402458

International Church Music Festival
Choral works by choirs from all over the world. Next festival 2005.
Tel: 01244 500962

Deva Triathlon
Rotary-run event in which ultra-fit people run, swim and cycle vast distances. Head for The Groves.

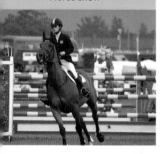

International Horse Show

Brass band

July
Raft Race
Fun for all as competitors splash on the river one Sunday in July.

Jazz and Blues Festival
All round the city for the whole month.
Tel: 01244 313400

Summer Music Festival
Two weeks of recitals, open-air concerts plus a fringe festival of every type of arts activity you can think of.
Tel: 01244 320700;
Fringe: 01244 320368

International Horse Show
Large, outdoor show-jumping event.
Tel: 01244 402330

August
Chester Regatta
Oldest rowing races in the world. Henley without the hooray-Henrys.
Tel: 0788 7881187

September
Weird world records
Attempts made to set a new mark for strange feats. Previous records include kites in the air and Rolls-Royces in a line.
Tel: 01244 320368

October
Literature Festival
Celebrity readings, work-shops and dining events throughout the month.
Tel: 01244 319985

November
Festival of trees
Annual celebration of tree decoration.
Tel: 01244 320368

December
Lantern Festivals
Dancing, street theatre and music on Thursday nights; late night shopping.
Tel: 01244 320368

Christmas Watch Parades
Medieval processions and bands on two Thursday nights to coincide with late-night shopping.
Tel: 01244 402478

The Cross at Christmas

CHESTER FOR KIDS

There's oodles of fun for children to enjoy in and around Chester.

The Roman heritage
The best place to start is The Grosvenor Museum (see page 40). Watch the video with its timeline countdown first, then visit the Roman galleries. Perhaps follow up by visiting Dewa Roman Experience (see page 37), where there are real remains and some good hands-on Roman games. Ask about the patrols – the chance for children to march around dressed in Roman gear.

City walls
Make sure your kids walk a stretch of the city walls. The best bit is the one from the Eastgate Arch to King Charles's Tower. Look for the anchor which marks the length from the Tower of Brunel's massive steam-ship, the SS *Great Eastern*.

River Dee
The other 'must-do' with children in Chester is to spend some time on the river. This might be a river trip combined with a city bus tour (see page 83) or, more exciting, hire a pedalo or a small boat.

Playground
Near the river is Grosvenor Park with a play area. In summer, it has a brilliant miniature steam railway (children aged four to nine are thrilled by it).

Chester Zoo
If you have the time, and your family likes animals, then Chester Zoo (see page 34) ought to be on your schedule. *Which?* magazine says that it's Britain's best zoo. Allow at least half a day and make sure you see Twilight World (the bat cave), the penguins, the apes and the Spirit of the Jaguar.

Dewa Roman Experience

Miniature railway,
Grosvenor Park

Cheshire Military Museum
The Grosvenor Museum

Roman soldier

Eating out with children

Good daytime places to eat with children include the child-friendly Chester Rows Café in Chester Visitor Centre (see page 69) and, if fine, Gabby's Crêperie (see page 69). Moules à Go-Go (see page 71) and La Tasca (see page 74) have a good reputation for their way with young diners.

Other city-centre options

Other things you might consider are the Cheshire Military Museum (see page 30), which is modern and has plenty of hands-on activities; the Town Crier (midday at the Cross; map C3); and the summer Ghost Hunter Tours (see page 80).

Out of Chester

Going further afield, your options multiply. The most popular choices with children are Blue Planet, with its underwater walk amongst the sharks (see page 89), and the Boat Museum at Ellesmere (see page 89). Cheshire Oaks (see page 58) is close to both of these places.

HAIL, CAESAR!

If you're in Chester on a summer Sunday, make sure you're at the Eastgate clock at midday to watch the changing of the Roman guard. It's an hour-long inspection and parade involving up to 25 soldiers in full military gear.

OUT OF TOWN

These are the places, all within easy reach of Chester, that people who stay in the city most enjoy visiting.

Stately homes and gardens

Tatton Park

22 miles north east of Chester, near Knutsford; A54 and A556

One of England's great estates, a neo-classical mansion and old Tudor hall surrounded by beautiful gardens and deer park. Hosts the annual RHS Flower Show in the north.
Tel: 01625 534400

Ness Gardens

Erddig

10 miles south of Chester, near Wrexham; A483 to Rhostyllen

This Georgian mansion is owned by The National Trust and is set in a delightful country park. It offers a special glimpse into life 'upstairs and downstairs' on a fine country estate.
Open: Sat–Wed, Apr–Nov
Tel: 01978 355314

Ness Gardens

6 miles north west of Chester at Neston, Wirral; A540

Botanic gardens containing plants, shrubs and trees from all over the world.
Tel: 0151 353 0123

Garden centres

Bridgemere Garden World

20 miles south east of Chester; A51 to Nantwich

For those with green fingers and money to spend; 5,000 plant varieties and 20 inspiring demo gardens.
Tel: 01270 521100

Stapeley Water Gardens

20 miles south east of Chester, near Nantwich; A51

The world's largest water-garden centre, home of the national collection of water lilies. Also a huge store stocking every kind of gear for anglers.
Tel: 01270 623868

Boat Museum

Catalyst

Grosvenor Garden Centre

2 miles south of Chester; near Nantwich; B5445 to Belgrave
Voted the Garden Centre of the Year in 2002.
Tel: 01244 625200

Wildlife
Blue Planet Aquarium

6 miles north of Chester; M53 to Ellesmere Port
The UK's ultimate underwater adventure. Take a voyage through the waters of the world and come eye-to-eye with over 2,000 fish, including one of the largest shark collections in Europe.
Tel: 0151 357 8800
Website: www.blueplanetaquarium.com

Art and architecture
Lady Lever Gallery

12 miles north east of Chester; A41 to Port Sunlight
Port Sunlight is a 19th-century garden village, built by Lord Leverhulme for his workers. The gallery includes paintings, furniture, porcelain, sculpture and tapestries.
Tel: 0151 478 4136

Science and technology
Boat Museum, Ellesmere Port

6 miles north of Chester; along the A53
The world's largest floating collection of canal craft, set in an historic dock complex. It includes many working pieces of heritage machinery.
Tel: 0151 355 5017
Website: www.boatmuseum.org.uk

Catalyst, Widnes

15 miles north of Chester; M56 then A557
Exciting hands-on, inter-active exploration of the impact of chemistry on our everyday lives.
Tel: 0151 420 1121
Website: www.catalyst.org.uk

Jodrell Bank

13 miles east of Chester; A54 to Holmes Chapel, then A535
Britain's foremost radio telescope. Visitors' Science centre, 3D theatre and planetarium.
Tel: 01477 571339
Website: www.jb.man.ac.uk/scicen

Jodrell Bank

Traditional street lamp

WHERE TO STAY

Chester has a wide selection of accommodation to suit all requirements and budgets. The list below will give you an idea of the range on offer, and includes places that represent excellent value in their price band. The £ symbols are an approximate guide for comparing the prices charged, which range from about £25 to over £100 per person per night. It's wise to check facilities and prices before you book.

Each year the city publishes the *Chester Visitor Guide* giving all the information you'll need. Send for it in advance if you want to know more about where you are staying. Chester's Tourism Information Service (see page 94) offers a friendly accommodation booking service in return for a small fee. Alternatively, you can plan your stay and book online via their website: www. chestertourism.com

The Chester Grosvenor
Eastgate Street; map D3
Without doubt Chester's most prestigious hotel, for its central location, its

private ownership by the city's patron family (see pages 16–18) and above all for the award-winning excellence of its accommodation, food and service. Built in 1865, it has a luxurious, traditional ambience, with 80 individually designed bedrooms. De luxe spa with luxury treatment rooms and thermal suite. For more about the restaurants, see page 71.
Tel: 01244 324024
Website: www.
chestergrosvenor.co.uk
£££££

Chester Crabwall Manor
Mollington, 3 miles from Chester

A beautiful 48-bedroomed country manor house 3 miles north-west of Chester. It may be some distance from the city centre, but the hotel's beautiful grounds are considerable compensation. Features superb leisure facilities, including a spa, long pool and aerobic studio.
Tel: 01244 851666
Website: www.
marstonhotels.com
£££££

Chester Moat House
Trinity Street, Chester; map B3
This recently built 160-bedroomed hotel has a superb location. It is

situated inside the city walls, yet enjoys lovely views over Chester's racecourse to the Welsh hills beyond. The decor is modern, with a pleasant honey-coloured warmth about the reception area and restaurant.
Tel: 01244 899988
Website: www.moathousehotels.com
££££

Green Bough Hotel
Hoole Road, Chester

An exclusive and award-winning luxury hotel on Hoole Road about a mile from the city centre. Each of its 16 rooms are individually styled with a modern Italian flavour. This hotel has won many accolades in recent years, not just for its comfort and service, but also for its food (see page 73).

Redland Hotel

Tel: 01244 326241
Website: www.greenbough.co.uk
££££

Redland Hotel
Hough Green, Chester

Despite its Victorian exterior, the wooden panelling and antique furniture of this friendly Hough Green hotel take it back another century or two, giving it a real olde-worlde feel. The 13 bedrooms are individually styled. If you fancy sleeping royally in a four-poster bed without paying a king's ransom for the privilege, this is the place.
Tel: 01244 671024
£££

The Limes
Hoole Road, Chester

This beautifully furnished, seven-bedroom guest house has won awards for the standard of its accommodation. The owners and staff aim to make your stay a home from home.
Tel: 01244 328239
Website: www.limeschester.btinternet.co.uk
££

Mitchells of Chester
Hough Green, Chester

Hough Green has a good selection of large Victorian guest houses. What makes this one special, apart from the friendly welcome (and the parrot) is the effort that has gone into the late-Victorian decor and furniture. Don't worry though – the facilities of the seven bedrooms aren't in the least bit Victorian! A very comfortable stay is assured.
Tel: 01244 679004
Website: www.mitchellsofchester.com
££

BaBa Guest House
Hoole Road, Chester

An award-winning family-run guest house in a large Victorian town house less than a mile from the city centre. It was the birthplace of the famous bomber pilot Leonard Cheshire V.C. You will

Mitchells of Chester

with a relaxing atmosphere of aromatherapy oils wafting through. It is very convenient for the city centre, either by bus or on foot. On-site parking for guests. Accepts non-smokers only.
Tel: 01244 323204
www.lavenderlodge.com
£

find lots of original features in each of its five spacious bedrooms.
Tel: 01244 315047
Website: www.babaguesthouse.co.uk
££

Buckingham House
Hough Green
Buckingham House is another one of Hough Green's large Victorian guest houses (it has five bedrooms). The owner's aim is to help you feel at home, even on rainy days! There are discounts for longer stays.
Tel: 01244 678600
£

Kilmorey Lodge
Hoole Road, Chester
A five-bedroomed Victorian guest house that stands out for the warmth of its welcome and the

consistent recommendations from previous guests. Family-run. For non-smokers only.
Tel: 01244 324306
£

Lavender Lodge
Hoole Road, Chester
This popular five-bedroom family-run guest house lives up to its name

BACKPACKERS
If you're on a really tight budget, Chester Backpackers (at 67 Boughton) offers basic accommodation and great value at around £15 per person per night.
Tel: 01244 400185

The Chester Grosvenor (page 91)

USEFUL INFORMATION

TOURIST INFORMATION

Tourist Information Centres

Chester Visitor Centre, Vicar's Lane, map E3 Extensive range of services, including accommodation booking, travel and events.
Tel: 01244 351609
Website: www.chestertourism.com

Similar services are also available at the Tourist Information Centre, Town Hall, Northgate Street, map C2.
Tel: 01244 402111

What's On

Look for *Chester Visitor Guide*, Chester Attractions and other leaflets available from Chester Visitor Centre and the Tourist Information Centre. Local newspapers also provide listings.

Guided Walks

For information and tour bookings for Pastfinder Tour; Walls Walk; Ghost Hunter Tours; Roman Soldier Wall Patrol (with legionary in full armour!); The Inn Tour; Literary tours; Cathedrals and Churches tours; Norman, Tudor or Victorian Chester tours; and Quiz tours contact:
Tourism Development Unit, Chester City Council, The Forum
Tel: 01244 402445 or 01244 402446
Website: www.chestertourism.com

Family Heritage

If you need help in tracing ancestors who lived in Chester and district (and also further afield), the first place to contact is Chester Community History and Heritage in Bridge Street.
Tel: 01244 402110
Website: www.chestercc.gov.uk/heritage/history/home.html

TRAVEL

Airport

Chester is served by two nearby airports – Manchester International Airport and Liverpool John Lennon Airport.
Tel: Manchester 0161 489 3000
Liverpool 08707 508484

Bus information

There is a regular National Express coach service between Manchester International Airport and Chester.
Tel: 08705 808080
Chester City Transport: bus services operate from Bus Exchange Point, Princess Street, behind Town Hall (map B2).
Tel: 01244 347452
Cheshire Bus: county and countryside services.
Tel: 01244 602666
Jones of Flint: day trips to North Wales.
Tel: 01352 733292
Busybus: day trips to North Wales.
Tel: 0870 874 1800

Shopmobility

For the loan of manual and electrically powered wheelchairs and scooters, Chester

Shopmobility Centre is located off Frodsham Street, in the Kaleyards car park (map D2). Two proofs of identification are required.
Tel: 01244 312626

Taxis
Black-cab taxi ranks outside the railway station and close to the Bus Exchange Point, next to the Town Hall (map C2).

Train information
Chester railway station is at the top of City Road. Shuttle bus every ten minutes from the station forecourt into the city centre; free on production of a rail ticket.
National Rail Enquiry Service (daily 24 hours)
Tel: 08457 484950

Park and Ride
map: see page 100
There are four park-and-ride sites around the Chester area, which are open Mon–Sat. Buses into the city run every ten minutes and are equipped with a low floor system for easy access. Car parking is free, and the return bus fare costs £1.20. The last buses back to the car parks leave at 18.20.

BANKS AND POST OFFICES
Abbey National, 59–61 Foregate Street; map E2
Barclays, 35 Eastgate Street; map D3 and 30 St Werburgh Street; map D2
Lloyds TSB, 8 Foregate Street; map E2
Lloyds TSB, 4 St John Street; map D3
HSBC, 47 Eastgate Street; map D2
NatWest, 33 Eastgate Street; map D3
Royal Bank of Scotland, 15 Foregate Street; map E2
Bank of Scotland, 117 Foregate Street; map E2
Yorkshire Bank, 38 Bridge Street; map C3

Post Offices
St John Street; map D3
Northgate Street; map C2
Watergate Street; map C3

SPORT
Northgate Arena, Victoria Road
Tel: 01244 380444
Christleton Sports Centre (2 miles from city centre)
Tel: 01244 336664

Almost all sports are catered for in Chester. For further details of specific requirements, contact the Tourist Information Centre.

EMERGENCIES
Fire, ambulance or police
Tel: 999

Police
Cheshire Constabulary, Castle Esplanade; map B5
Tel: 01244 350000

Countess of Chester Hospital
Liverpool Road; includes accident and emergency
Tel: 01244 365000

Dental emergencies
City Walls Medical Centre, St Martin's Way
Tel: 01244 356802

24-hour petrol station
Tesco at Broughton Park (10–12 mins along A55 towards North Wales)
Tel: 01244 587300

Total, 302 Sealand Road, Deeside (15–20 mins drive along A548 towards North Wales)
Tel: 01244 378945

24-hour breakdown
MJB Commercials, Deeside Industrial Estate, Deeside, Clwyd
Tel: 01244 288451

INDEX

CITY-BREAK GUIDES

These full-colour guides come with stunning new photography capturing the special essence of some of Britain's loveliest cities. Each is divided into easy-reference sections where you will find something for everyone – from walk maps to fabulous shopping, from sightseeing highlights to keeping the kids entertained, from recommended restaurants to tours and trips ... and much, much more.

BATH

Stylish and sophisticated – just two adjectives that sum up the delightful Roman city of Bath, which saw a resurgence of popularity in Georgian times and in the 21st century is once again a vibrant and exciting place to be.

CAMBRIDGE

Historic architecture mingles with hi-tech revolution in the university city of Cambridge, where stunning skylines over surrounding fenland meet the style and sophistication of modern city living.

CHESTER

Savour the historic delights of the Roman walls and charming black-and-white architecture, blending seamlessly with the contemporary shopping experience that make Chester such an exhilarating city.

OXFORD

City and university life intertwine in Oxford, with its museums, bookstores and all manner of sophisticated entertainment to entice visitors to its hidden alleyways, splendid quadrangles and skyline of dreaming spires.

STRATFORD

Universally appealing, the picturesque streets of Stratford draw visitors back time and again to explore Shakespeare's birthplace, but also to relish the theatres and stylish riverside town that exists today.

YORK

A warm northern welcome and modern-day world-class shops and restaurants await you in York, along with its ancient city walls, Viking connections and magnificent medieval Minster rising above the rooftops.

Jarrold Publishing, Healey House, Dene Road, Andover, Hampshire, SP10 2AA, UK
Sales: 01264 409206
Enquiries: 01264 409200
Fax: 01264 334110
e-mail: heritagesales@jarrold-publishing.co.uk
website: www.britguides.com

MAIN ROUTES IN AND OUT OF CHESTER

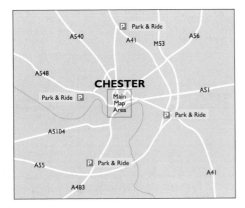

Park and ride services leave regularly for central Chester from:

Boughton Heath Park and Ride
At the junction of the A55 and A41

Sealand Road Park and Ride
On the A548

Upton (The Zoo) Park and Ride
On the A41

Wrexham Road Park and Ride
On the A483

See page 95 for further details